BACKWARDS & FORWARDS

my journey through Africa

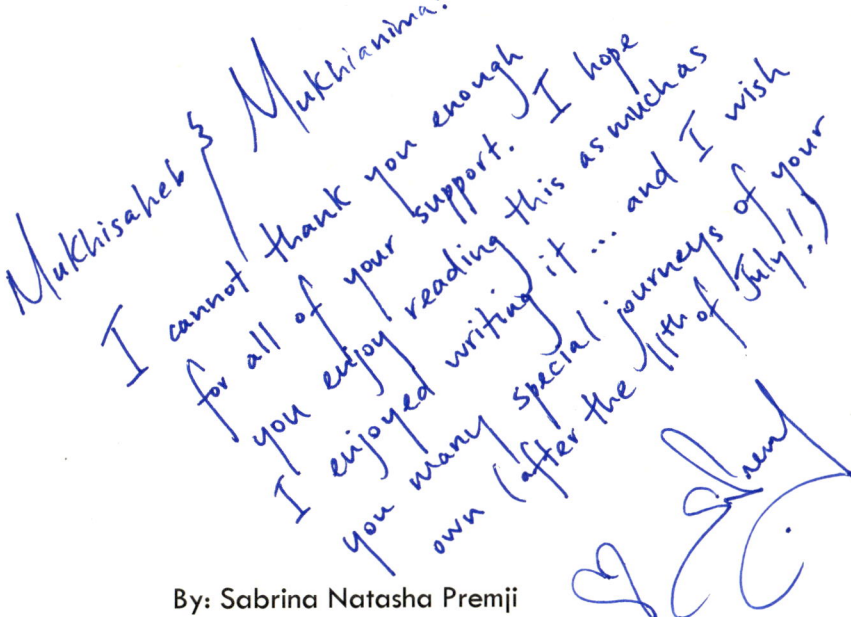

By: Sabrina Natasha Premji

Copyright © 2012 – Sabrina Natasha Premji

Premji Productions

in association with

SETT Publications (editing)

All rights reserved. No part of this book may be used or reproduced in any manner whatsoever without the express written consent of the Publishers. Written in Kenya. Edited in Canada. Printed in the United States of America.

ISBN: 978-1-300-08286-6

Author: Premji, Sabrina Natasha

Edition: 2nd edition

Citation:

Premji, Sabrina Natasha. "Backwards & Forwards." Web log post. Backwards & Forwards: A Journey Through Africa. 2011-2012. Web. 22 Mar. 2012. <http://sabrinapremji.wordpress.com>.

Chapters

"Toto, I've a feeling we're not in Kansas anymore"

Home

A Canadian girl's survival guide to fending off Kenyan men.

A day of thanks

Dubai: concrete desert where dreams are made of

"Run Forest Run..."

Wait, you don't have a housemaid?

Toenails are so overrated

Addictions

People may just surprise you

"Valentine's Day is not a real holiday"

The day I figured out what I want to do when I'm all grown up

Ode to the matatu driver

It's raining, it's pouring...

Just have faith

One year ago

The genetic lottery

Authenticity

Silence

Moments

My new year's resolution

From ideas to impact

The only thing worse than the smell of a dead rat is...

The next generation of social entrepreneurs

Foreword

I couldn't wait. I impatiently watched my inbox everyday asking myself when it would come. That email that made my heart jump and my eyes widen. Sometimes it took only a week, other times a month, and from time to time I thought it would never come again. Like countless others, I waited for the next installment of Sabrina's blog.

She has an amazing way of transporting readers – describing her surroundings, her feelings, and her thoughts in a way that makes you feel as though you are right by her side. It made each installment a joy to read.

This book is a testament to the experiences Sabrina has encountered. To the utopian world that she seeks to create. To her potential to inspire people. It is proof – proof that deep down, Sabrina is a writer.

This publication is just the beginning. As a natural storyteller, I see Sabrina continue to share her insights about sustainable development with her hundreds, perhaps thousands, of followers around the world.

And so I continue to wait. But no longer am I watching my inbox for the next blog post. Now I wait for her next book.

- Afzal Habib

Prologue

We're all moving. Each one of us. We're in a frantic race to the finish line, striving to meet deadlines and deliver on commitments. We're moving and we're chasing, as the years pass us by. And then something happens – an idea, a conversation, an opportunity – that causes us to shift our sails and steer ourselves in a completely new direction. One significant moment that changes everything.

For me, that moment came on April 1st, 2010 – April Fools' Day, of all days. Sitting in the library studying for my final set of University exams, I received an email saying I had been awarded a prestigious international development fellowship. And from that moment on, my life has never been the same.

As a recipient of the International Development Management Fellowship (funded by the Aga Khan Foundation Canada and Canadian International Development Agency), I spent four weeks with seventeen exceptional people in our country's capital of Ottawa for an intensive 'crash course' in development. We engaged in discussions with world-renowned experts who walked us through theories of market development, systems-based thinking and monitoring and evaluation, and applied those theories in case studies presented to top-notch executives. Some few weeks later, I found myself in the middle of a rural East African village checking the HIV/AIDS status of community members. Talk about a 360.

My fellowship in Mombasa followed by a contract at the Aga Khan University in Nairobi, Kenya were transformational. My understanding of life shifted dramatically and for the first time, I became aware of the world outside my comfy North American bubble. I witnessed the perils of those who lie at the bottom-of-the-pyramid, and the small victories they achieve every single day. I learned to value every single drop of water, and celebrated days when the electricity did not cut out. I connected with people on a level that transcended language and engaged with communities that taught me more about life than any University course could. I fell in love. I became an excellent barterer in the local language of *Kiswahili*. I learned what it was like to feel unsafe and terribly alone. I became a proud mother of a baby elephant. I experienced the challenges and limitations of the development sector and advocated for innovation to traditional approaches of program design and implementation. I was reminded every single day to be grateful.

This book is a collection of my blog posts over the twenty-two months I spent living and working in Kenya. The views expressed do not represent CIDA, the Aga Khan Development Network or any other organization.

Many thanks are offered to my colleagues at the Community Health Department, Aga Khan University and district of Kaloleni, with special acknowledgment to Dr. Michaela Mantel, Dr. Robert Armstrong, Dr. Mushtaq Ahmed, Professor Yasmin Amarsi, Dr. Raheem Dhanani, Mr. Sisawo Konteh, Dr. Amyn Lakhani, Ms. Asifa Nurani and Dr. Sylver Quevedo. I thank you for your exceptional mentorship.

Thank you to my family and friends for your positive energy and notes of encouragement — they were beacons of light on some of the darkest days. To the Nicholls, I cannot thank you enough for adopting me into your family and giving me a sense of *home*.

Mom, Dad — thank you for your unwavering support through muffled Skype conversations, not getting mad at me for ridiculously expensive long-distance calls and for always challenging me to dream big. And to my love, Afzal — you envisioned this book before I ever could. Thanks for being my everything.

August 19, 2010

"Toto, I've a feeling we're not in Kansas anymore"

I am sitting at a departure gate in the Moi International Airport in Mombasa waiting to board my flight back to Nairobi. My 3 week old Birks sit tired on the ground beside me, beaten and scathed from hiking through rural Kenyan villages. My hair is curly and disheveled from the humidity – a trademark here on the Coast. I close my eyes and can picture my adopted goat – my mbuzi. The only words fluttering through my mind are those of a wise Kenyan man I met today – "Arriving in Mombasa is a wedding; leaving Mombasa is a funeral."

Perhaps I should back up a bit. I arrived in Kenya 1 week ago – a place that I will call home for the next 8 months. I wish I could say I had a more interesting adventure to this side of the world. That my luggage was accidently directed to Alaska or I dropped a slipper in the Amsterdam airport which was promptly returned by Prince Charming himself. But alas, nothing noteworthy to report.

This past week in Nairobi has kept me busy. With meetings at the Aga Khan Foundation East Africa, Nation Media Group, Aga Khan University, Aga Khan Development Network and frequent trips to the Immigration Office, there has been no time for jet lag to peep its naughty head.

If only there was a way to send you all one-way tickets to Nairobi to see what I'm seeing, to experience what I'm experiencing. Words don't seem to do justice to this bustling cosmopolitan. Pull up an image of Africa in your head – picture the roads, the people, the dress. Have you got it? Great, now scrunch up that image and throw it away. Nairobi is completely unlike what I imagined it to be. It's modern and progressive. Blackberry and Lexus billboards plaster the cityscape while men in three-piece suits line the streets. Rihanna and the Black Eyed Peas are heard raring through the local nightclubs – although slow love songs from the 90s seem to be the music choice for most. Security guards with AK47s are permanent fixtures in malls and grocery stores. And the driving – oh goodness, the driving! There are cars, motorcycles, matatus[1], pedestrians, lions (just kidding)...everywhere, traveling in every conceivable direction. Rules of the road simply don't exist.

Just down the road, about an hour's flight away, lies Mombasa – an escape from the craziness of the city. I spent two jam-packed days in this oasis off the coast and instantly connected with its laidback, 'time is elastic and must be stretched' spirit.

Most of my time in Mombasa was spent in the field, touring projects of the Aga Khan Foundation's Coastal Rural Support Programme (CRSP). 4 villages. 4 projects. Impact: immeasurable. Getting to these

---

[1] Local multi-person transport vans that blare top 40 music throughout the city

communities was a feat in itself: Hours on bumpy, winding, dirt roads – and in many cases, hiking through untamed fields – to reach completely rural villages with no running water or sustainable sources of energy. Villages completely isolated from the rest of humanity – and yet, thriving through the support of CRSP. CRSP assisted one community in using innovative irrigation techniques to harvest their crops, enabling them to enter the local cash crop market system. A farmer in another village experimented with cross-breeding different species of goats, creating a hybrid offspring with significantly greater value in the market. A neighbouring community initiated an agro-forestry project yielding eucalyptus trees, the trunks of which can be sold and used to construct power lines. CRSP has made a tremendous impact on the 190 Kenyan villages it works in, empowering communities to develop strategies to, quite literally, dig their way out of poverty. It was beyond incredible to see their work in action.

There is truth to the words of that wise fellow – leaving Mombasa is indeed a funeral. I plan to camp out at the Nairobi immigration office until my fingers have been printed, my photo taken, my passport stamped and a work permit in hand. Until then, my fingers and toes shall remain crossed!

August 26, 2010

I have arrived

Every hero has a signature superpower — his claim to fame that takes him from geek to God. Spiderman has his spidey-sense, Superman can move faster than a speeding bullet, Jack Bauer is... just Jack Bauer, and Batman — well, it's a toss-up between the Batmobile and his well-fitting tights.

Although nowhere near superhero status (save for the well-fitting tights), I too have developed a toolbox to ward off evil.

Exhibit A: Doom

The day I moved into my flat, my landlady (affectionately known as Mama Rosy), gave me a bottle of Doom and wished me well. Naively, I assumed she was wishing me a warm welcome to Mombasa or perhaps, wishing me a good first day of work. Oh no, no! It's painfully clear now that Mama Rosy was wishing me success in my battle against the cockroaches.

Half-asleep and barely able to see, I staggered to the bathroom my first morning at the flat to brush my teeth, only to find a cockroach the size of my index finger resting on the bathroom floor. I shrieked at its sight, but the little roach stayed motionless, probably amused by this cowardly Canadian. I contemplated my options, drafted a mental pro-con list then settled on a plan of attack – I'd step on it. I ran to my room, grabbed one of my shoes (poor Birks, oh what I've put them through!), narrowed in on my target, realized I couldn't see my target, ran back to my room, put on my glasses, then…ever so gently, I raised my hand and…WHACK! My shoe hit the ground hard as the little scoundrel flew out of sight. It was a flying cockroach – that nasty little bugger. I ran back to my room, grabbed the bottle of Doom and sprayed down the entire bathroom until the rascal was no more. Sabrina: 1, Cockroach: 0.

Exhibit B: A Mop

There are very few things I hate in life. Although I strongly dislike Peyton Manning and I'm not particularly fond of ironing, I can't say I <u>hate</u> them – it just seems too strong of a word. But I can safely say, I hate Tom.

Tom is a dog. I don't know much about dogs. I couldn't tell you his breed or age. What I do know is Tom is a big dog, and along with his 4 other canine friends, he is the last defence mechanism between a thief and Mama Rosy's house. Locks can be picked, gates can be jumped over, security guards can be bribed, but dogs – they're loyal to the house.

Tom on the other hand is loyal to no one but himself. In my 8 days in Mombasa, he has destroyed the backyard furniture, brought two young children to hysterical tears, broken fine china, kept the entire block awake with his midnight barking and has nearly bitten my hand off… twice.

My defence against Tom is an old, grungy mop. As I walk up the stairs from my flat to the main property, I bang the mop against the ground. The sound keeps him off my case until I reach the security guard who then cusses Tom in an unending stream of Swahili words. If only werewolf-like Tom would one day morph into Jacob Black…

Exhibit C: Anjale

You know the nursery rhyme 'Three Blind Mice'? Story goes, three blind mice went after the farmer's wife who cut off their tails with a carving knife. I don't have a carving knife but I do have Anjale, Mama Rosy's gatekeeper. Upon sight of a mouse in my bedroom two nights ago, I screamed bloody Mary until Anjale came to my rescue and hit the poor bugger dead with a broomstick. I rather not delve into the details of the story — how I stood on a chair in tears throughout the entire hunt, how the mouse scurried over my foot while it was trying to make a valiant escape, how I haven't had a wink of sleep ever since.

On the bright side...

I may not have an invisibility cloak or the ability to fly, but with Anjale, my mop and Doom in hand, I'm ready to take on anything that comes my way. Mombasa, I have arrived!

September 10, 2010

Home

For as long as I've known him, my brother has been an exceptional hockey goalie. Some of my fondest childhood memories are watching him slide across the crease, making spectacular glove saves, stopping every puck that came his way. Whether it was six o'clock in the morning or eleven o'clock at night, when Shayne suited up and stood between those two posts, he was home.

When you're halfway around the world and terribly far away from home, you begin to search for that feeling of absolute comfort, a place to just be. In my one month in Mombasa, I've found home in two very different places: the field and the gym.

As a Community Health Fellow with the Aga Khan Health Service, I get to dip my feet in a number of projects, one of which is conducting verbal autopsies in rural villages to identify the primary causes of child mortality. The days are long, the journeys are treacherous, the outcomes are unpredictable. But once I reach that rural dispensary clinic and look into the eyes of a child who has been given life-saving malaria medication or see the smile on a mother's face who has survived a pregnancy because she had access to a trained midwife... I'm home.

I love everything about the field. I love how it puts life into perspective. Take for example the story of Elizabeth, a middle-aged nurse working in a clinic in the village of Matuga. She arrives at the centre, a building no larger than a basketball key, at the crack of dawn to a queue of patients who've saved up enough money, or sold enough goats, to afford medical care. When the sun goes down, signalling the end of the work day (because there's no electricity to power light), Elizabeth gets an urgent message – a pregnant woman has gone into labour and requires immediate attention. Elizabeth assembles a kit of supplies, spends the night delivering a baby, reaches home just in time to dress her child for school and heads back to the clinic – greeted again by a long queue of patients. She believes with every fibre of her being that God will reward her in the next life. That's perspective.

In the field, excessive materialism, the lust for fame and need for power are supplanted by hope, generosity and a humility like no other. Everywhere I go, I hear the word *karibu*, or 'welcome'. *Karibu* Mombasa, *karibu* chai, *karibu*, *karibu*, *karibu*. When I say *asante* or thank you, they return by saying *karibu* again, to which I say *asante* prompting another *karibu* – before you know it, you're stuck in one of those chicken or egg paradoxes! I love the raw emotions of the field – the hope of a mother who has given up everything to send her children to school; the agony of a husband who has lost his wife due to complications in childbirth; the innocence of a child who clings to his mother's back, unbeknownst of any other world but the one he sees day in and day out. Every emotion, good and bad, has its place here. Most of all, I love what the field does to me – it infuses me with a sense of vibrancy and heightens my thirst to make a sustainable difference. The field has become my sanctuary.

If a monitoring and evaluation framework were to be conducted on international placements, a good indicator of integration could be when you're considered a 'regular' somewhere. When I'm not in the field, I'm a frequent flyer at the local athletic club. I grapevine, crunch, and sweat like the best of 'em in my aerobics class conducted in Swahili by a bootcamp instructor from hell. If only I could learn to say "I'm too tired" or "I'm not that flexible" in Swahili! Pascal and Joseph, my hunky personal trainers, are the cherry on top. Pascal started by giving me a 3lb weight for bicep curls, which I promptly switched for a 20lb dumbbell. Clearly he's doesn't know what us Canadian girls are made of!

I may be a million miles away from Canada but by conversing with a nurse at a rural dispensary or doing push-ups at the local gym, I somehow lose myself... and magically, home doesn't feel so far away.

P.S. In case you were wondering about the jungle that is my flat, turns out we're battling an army — 3 days, 3 mice including one found dead in a jewellery box. Gross! I've moved out of the flat into another room within the same property — no mouse sightings to report as of yet...

September 28, 2010

A Canadian girl's survival guide to fending off Kenyan men

I am a firm believer in the power of a well put-together outfit. After all, a slipper can land you a husband (Cinderella taught us that!), a cloak can solemnly keep you up to no good (think Harry Potter!) and after last week's events, I'm certain that a ring can indeed combat an entire army of Kenyan men.

I'm not sure what's in the Mombasa water, but it's turning all the men a little crazy. Never have I been chased, courted or pursued more than I have in the last week.

Chapter 1:

It all began like any other ordinary day — I woke up glued to my sheets from the sweltering Mombasa heat, fended off cunning monkeys trying to steal my breakfast, said jambo to cockadoodle-doo-ing roosters on my walk up to the main road and hopped on a matatu to ride to work. And this is where things got a bit awry. Not every day do I sit beside a young, dashing Arab man who charmingly canoodles his way into my heart and phonebook. Before you ask me for the wedding date, I must regretfully submit that Mr. Matatu Man was no Prince Charming at all. 24 hours, 11 calls and 12 texts later, this bloke needed to go... and go fast. It took a nasty call from a friend to rid of the persistent player. Lesson learned from Mr. Matatu Man: don't ever give your phone number to anyone, even if they look like Hrithik Roshan. Duly noted.

I did keep one particularly memorable SMS just for kicks:

> *"When you breathe, you respire... Wah wah*
> *When you stop breathing, you expire...Wah wah"*

Romantic eh?

Chapter 2:

The Community Health Department is a revolving door for visitors from the community and other partner organizations. Since I sit closest to the meeting room, I proudly greet these guests in my finest display of broken Kiswahili. Bad idea.

Apparently, my jambo was misinterpreted as an invitation for romantic courtship by one visitor, who subsequently created a love potion to woo me. Love potions in Africa are transmitted through long, firm handshakes – something I wish I had known earlier, as I happened to meet said Potion Man at a workshop last week and was bewildered by his need to shake my hand every time I saw him. Let it be known that I have doused my hands in an unhealthy amount of sanitizer ever since. Take that love potion!

Lesson learned from Potion Man: don't say jambo to any man under any circumstance. Who knows what spell he might cast on you!

Chapter 3:

It's a fact – you're not Mombasan until you ride a matatu. I'm usually the only foreigner on the matatu, ergo I get stared at... a lot. Rather than bust out the awkward turtle, I use it as an opportunity to look out the window and take in the sights and smells of town. This past week, I made a blunder; a mistake so big, I am embarrassed to admit it on a forum like this. I'm a seasoned matatu-rider, it's inexcusable that I committed an offense of such magnitude. I made eye contact. There, I said it. I made eye contact. A middle-aged, hefty-set gentleman stared and I glanced back — gosh, I should have known better. Before you know it, I was invited to go to the beach with the Jolly Green Giant the following weekend. I survived the matatu ride unscathed but lesson learned: sunglasses are your best friend on a matatu.

Chapter 4:

Lunchtime aerobics classes at the local athletic club have become a daily ritual. I must admit, after an hour of sweating like a never-ending fountain in an AC-less, fan-less room, I'm not in my most attractive state. Somehow, God knows how, my chest presses must have caught the eye of one potential suitor who endeavoured to track down my name and place of work. How I know this? From Mr. Gym Guy himself, when he showed up at my office last week and proudly spoke of his taxing quest to find me. I think he was thoroughly unimpressed by my apparent lack of enthusiasm. The gatekeepers at the hospital have been given the heads up should he show up again, but it's safe to assume my look of utter shock was enough to scare him off for good. Lesson learned: sweat can apparently be attractive. Embrace it.

A week of men left, right and centre led me straight to the market to buy a fake wedding ring. It cost nothing more than a few dollars, but is doing the trick to shield off anything and anyone with an XY chromosome. In case anyone asks, my husband's name is Jacob and we are living happily ever after in a castle far far away.

October 11, 2010

A day of thanks

Nashukuru. Definitely my most favourite Swahili word. I love the way it rolls off your tongue – *nashukuru*. I love the way it instantly grounds you and puts life into perspective. It's one of those words that cannot be said, but rather must be felt with every part of your being. *Nashukuru* means 'I give thanks' and is used to express gratitude for all that life has bestowed upon us. Since it's Thanksgiving back home, it only seems fitting to give thanks, as per Premji-family tradition. Here is my own nashukuru list:

I am thankful for Elizabeth, a 4 year old, HIV positive girl I met at an orphanage just outside town. Elizabeth is living in a country where the stigma of HIV rings loudly. Without parents to provide school fees, it is unlikely she will have the chance to get a solid education. Uneducated, stigmatized and destitute – the harsh reality that likely awaits this beautiful, wide-eyed child. And yet as she played with my hair and told me of her dream to become a teacher when she grows up, she showed me the beauty and innocence of being a child. A time where anything is possible. I'm thankful for Elizabeth for reminding me why I do what I do. *Nashukuru.*

I am thankful for Chamutu, our office assistant, who scurries over to my desk every morning and says "*Rafiki karibu chai*". Welcome to tea time. Chamutu has spent the last thirty years perfecting the art of chai making – he is indeed a master of the trade. In that moment, sipping away at arguably the world's best cup of chai, I forget about skyrocketing TB cases, limited medical resources and the rising infant mortality rate. All the world's problems seem to disappear with Chamutu's chai. *Nashukuru.*

I was recently involved in a focus group discussion conducted to understand the socio-economic and cultural barriers preventing pregnant women in rural villages from delivering in a health care facility. One young woman, not much older than me, poignantly described her experience delivering at home: "*Wakati mwengine nyumba ya uzazi inashinda kutoka baada ya kuzaa, ikitokea hivyo tunafunga uzi uliounganishwa na jiwe katika kitovu ili itoke kwa haraka*". Translation: "Sometimes the placenta is retained in the womb so I tie the placenta using a string attached to a stone so that it can come out very fast". I shake at the thought of this – removing your own placenta with a rock just after giving birth. I am grateful for having grown up in a country where access to quality health care is a basic right. *Nashukuru.*

I am thankful for Mr. Agendo, who has converted his house and donated nearly all his income to the building of a primary school. His desire to give the children in his village a better life surmounts the financial constraints and emotional exhaustion of taking power into his own hands.

I am thankful for George, a 103 year old tortoise who has taught me that time is really a very relative concept.

I am thankful for life sending such incredible people my way and within a matter of weeks, transforming them from friend-quaintances into family: Jennifer, our house lady, whose face lights up when I return home from work in the evening; Anjale, our gatekeeper, who declares in his most well-rehearsed English, "I had a good day", every time I see him (this often happens multiple times a day and it makes me smile every time!); Fatma and Supria, the askaris at my work, who prayed for me when I was sick in hospital with a salmonella parasite[2]; Francis, the aerobics instructor, who has taught me how to shake my booty in ways I didn't think were possible; and a crew of friends that would bend over backwards for each other.

Thanksgiving Day may be a foreign concept here, but I'm beginning to think that every day ought to be a day of thanks. In my world, every day is Nashukuru Day.

---

[2] Affectionately referred to as Pete the Parasite

23

November 2, 2010

Dubai: concrete desert where dreams are made of

I love Mombasa – the people, the language, the culture, the heat. Everything about this place radiates happiness. But after 10 weeks in Africa, I was craving a soft bed, laundered clothes, a hot shower and most of all, a salad. So I packed my bags and flew to Dubai for a week, no passing "Go", no collecting $200.

Coming from the land of mosquitoes, Swahili and chapatis, it was quite the culture shock landing in the middle of perfection. That's what Dubai really is in essence – a perfectionist. It strives to have the tallest towers, the biggest malls, the classiest hotels, the newest technology. But underneath any perfectionist is insecurity, a vulnerability of some sort. Behind the facade of BMWs and Prada handbags lies an absolute fear of failing and an inequality unlike no other.

Case example – an entire ocean was excavated and turned into a fortress of five-star hotels and villas fit for a king in the span of a few months. What isn't seen are the thousands of workers imported from surrounding countries who worked night and day to create paradise from scratch, receiving little compensation of which most was sent to their families back home. Their sacrifice to leave their world in the hopes of a more prosperous life has rendered little in return; The 'blood men' — disenchanted workers who stand fixated by the side of the road and wait for an opportune moment to haul themselves in front of a flashy car. The financial compensation their family receives for their death — for the driver would be convicted for murder under Dubai's unspoken 'guilty until proven innocent' law — serves as enough of a motivation to engage in such a horrendous act; The lack of freedom to retire in Dubai — work permits for expats are declined after the age of 55, in essence to keep the city free from an aging population and the burden of disease that comes with it; The lack of privacy — every text message, every email, every BBM passes through a government server and can be monitored at any time.[3]

Freudian analysis aside, here are the highlights of my time in Dubai:

- Celebrated an exquisite belated Canadian Thanksgiving: we made perogies and pumpkin pie from scratch.[4]
- Mastered the art of bargaining in Old Dubai. The trick — pull out a calculator and frantically add, subtract, multiply and divide numbers until the bewildered clerk literally begs you take their merchandise and leave the store.
- Experienced the Ismaili Centre in Dubai — arguably one of the most peaceful places on this side of the world.

---

[3] Side note: Mom, Dad – sorry for the complete lack of communication. Skype is banned in Dubai. I promise, I did not rusn away with an Arab Sheikh...for long anyways.

[4] Future husband, it is with great delight that I can now put more than a peanut butter sandwich on my list of culinary talents!

- Bought a belly dancing outfit. Figuring out what to do with it? Whole different story.
- Was greeted by every salesman at the spice market by the same two lines: where are you from? And after pulling out a spice from their collection and making you smell it, they'd ask do you know what this is? I answered pepper every time. 1 for 12 is not bad — it's better than the Leaf's chances of winning the Stanley Cup!
- Rode a camel
- Rode up and down sand dunes in the desert that literally defied all sense of gravity.

- Ate loads and loads of salad
- Shopped til' I dropped — apparently it is possible to max out a credit card in a day. Who knew?
- Comforted a flying-phobic runner on the Kenyan National team who was returning from competitions in Morocco, on a very turbulent airplane ride back to Mombasa. Was later invited to live with him but politely declined.

Dubai was exactly what I needed to spice things up again. I have come back to Mombasa tanned, re-energized, and recommitted to making the most of my time remaining in Kenya. In fact, I've made a list. 85 things left to do by March 2011.

My personal favourites:

#11 Master the super complicated hip/belly thrust move in Francis' aerobics class
#20 High-five a matatu conductor
#31 Learn how to make a really good cup of chai
#36 Avoid getting malaria
#39 Learn how to drive a standard car
#53 Make a difference
#67 Figure out what really goes down at our neighbour's house[5]
#68 Understand Kenya
#78 Make Mombasa feel like home.

The list is quite daunting, I may need a couple of extra years here. Just sayin'...

---

[5] Our theory is it's a pig slaughtering house but with the sounds we hear every night, I wouldn't be surprised if they have a whole jungle in there!

November 22, 2010

"Run Forest Run…"

I woke up one morning last week and it hit me like a stack of textbooks to the head – I'm in Africa. Three simple words, and yet somehow they rang to a different tune last week. I'm in Africa. No longer a tourist nor an eager graduate wanting to check off 'see Africa' on her list of things to do before she turns 30. I live here. Kenya is my home. My God.

The 'oh my gosh' feeling marks the end of the honeymoon period, according to Randy Weekes, intercultural effectiveness consultant extraordinaire. What follows the honeymoon high depends entirely on the road taken. Some remove their lenses of wonder and begin to see a place for all its imperfections – the corruption, the inefficiency, the inequality. It's a dangerous path to pursue, as losing a sense of curiosity can quickly deteriorate into grumpiness, escape fantasies and an us-vs.-them syndrome. Others choose to let go. What defined an individual back home – whether it was libraries or family time or football – no longer exist, forcing the individual to embrace a new reality, to create a new world, to re-invent himself. As challenging and emotionally exhausting as it may be, this process of letting go can be the greatest gift of all.

I took a less sophisticated approach to the 3-month mark — I ran... literally. I was tired of being stared at everywhere I went — so I ran. I was tired of being approached for money, from gatekeepers at the hospital to children on the street — so I ran. I was tired of having to walk on eggshells, for in a community as small as Mombasa, your every move is analyzed and discussed in public forums. Think Gossip Girl, but worse. I was tired of the heat that knocks the energy out of you within minutes of being outside, leaving you in a stream of sweat — so I ran. I was tired of men objectifying women and proposing marriage in spite of already having two wives — so I ran. I was tired of being suspicious of people's intentions, whether to interpret their friendliness as genuine or a fearless shot at a Canadian passport. I was tired of the sun dictating where and when I could venture out alone, selfishly taking a piece of my independence and need to do things on my own — so I ran. I was tired of parasites and mosquitoes who attack without any respite.

I was tired, so I ran.

It couldn't have been more than half an hour around the block, but it was cathartic. Liberating, in fact. It emptied my head of everything — every insecurity, every fear, every uncertainty — leaving me open to embrace this new world. It tucked Canada a little further away into the crevices of my heart, making a wee bit more room for Africa to find its place.

P.S.

Speaking of Africa, I'm happy to note that good progress has been made on the Mombasa bucket list.

#3 Learn how to swim — I'm proud to say I can now do a remixed version of a doggy paddle and a front crawl.

#30 Figure out what the big fuss is about soccer and Liverpool (as long as I live, soccer shall remain as soccer not football, no matter how many crazy Kenyans tell me otherwise!) It took one look at Torres and I became a religious Liverpool fan; you'll never walk alone.

#67 Figure out what really goes on at our neighbour's house — Turns out they're involved in a pig slaughtering and fishing business. How do I know this? I had a basketball date with one of my neighbours who had to take a rain check because, according to his text: "I have to go to the navy base 'cause my divers have been mistaken as pirates." Nope, not a drunk text at 3 in the morning. He was dead serious.

#8 Visit Tumaini HIV/AIDS Orphanage – my regular Saturday hangout spot. These children are beautiful; I may pull an Angelina Jolie and bring them all back home with me.

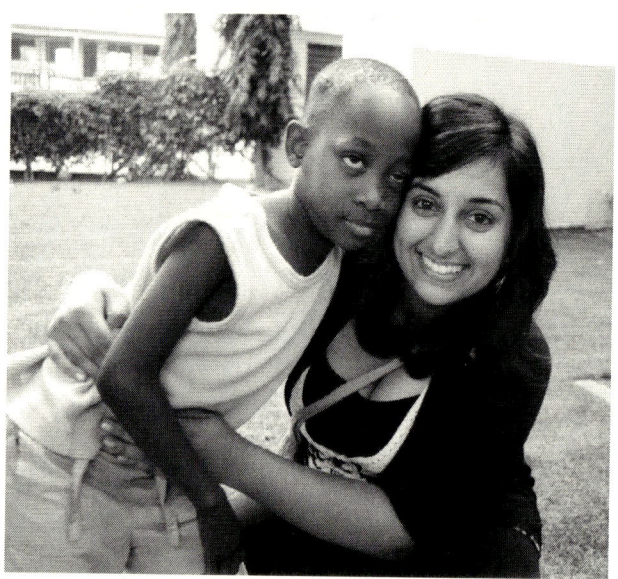

January 14, 2011

Wait, you don't have a housemaid?

I really like the start of a new year. There's something liberating about having a completely fresh start; to resolve to do the things you haven't made time to do (or recover from the things you shouldn't have done during the break prior!). And every year, there are a few of those sneaky resolutions that manage to make the list again. I don't know whether it's the African water or the Mombasa heat, but for the very first time in my entire life, I have a newbie on my resolution list that I still can't believe made the cut. This year, I resolve to be domesticated.

Every flower has a root and I suppose this one stems from moving into my own flat last week. With the excitement of living on my own, I completely forgot...that I would be living on my own... in Africa. A place where dishwashers are unheard of, clothes are meant to be hung and power goes out more times than it stays on. And I'm afraid of lighting a match. Interesting does not even begin to describe it.

Here is a glimpse at my first week in my new flat:

Day 1: I stepped into my apartment and there waiting for me in the centre of the kitchen floor was a big, fat, hairy cockroach. Silly cockroach, I did not *karibu* you. I must admit for a moment, I felt a bit sorry for the bugger because it was laying on its back with its legs frantically moving in the air. Whether he was having difficulty getting up or simply enjoying his afternoon yoga, I have yet to ascertain. I booked it out of the flat while the repairman hanging about did the needful.

Day 2: Living in the house is tough enough, who would have thought leaving the house ought to be just as hard? After ensuring every light was turned off and all windows were closed tight (lest forbid a creepy crawly or extremely slim robber found its way in), I left the house and tried locking up. Tried, being the operative word. No matter how many times I fiddled with the lock, or said magic abracadabra-type words, the door would just not close. My very elderly, slightly deaf, non-English speaking neighbour must have heard my struggles and sauntered over to assist. Without saying a word, he stuck his rear-end against the door, using one hand on the handle, one hand on the key and his *ahem* backside as leverage against the door. And just like that, the lock slipped quickly into place. Why didn't someone just tell me you have to put your butt into it? Done and done. I haven't had trouble with my door ever since.

Day 3: I like to play. Moving into a new house is like going to a playground, with new gadgets to discover and levers to pull. Every switch I found in the flat did something — it was Newton's Third Law of Physics at its finest. That is, all except for one. I flicked, I switched but nothing seemed to happen. I figured the switch was defective (or simply decorative) and forgot all about it. A few hours later, I heard pools of water crashing against the pavement, almost like an ocean had suddenly appeared from thin air. I ran to the balcony only to find the water tank on my roof heaping litres of water below, while a neighbour stood with her hands on her hips cluck-clucking in a foreign language. Turns out I inadvertently pumped up too much water[6]. My handy

---

[6] ...so if the Indian ocean suddenly runs dry, I take full responsibility.

repairman was able to stop the flood but his powers were rendered useless at altering the bad reputation I had created for myself in the new neighbourhood. And it's only Day 3.

Day 4: Sunday! My one day to indulge in the absolute pleasure of sleeping in. However, my REM cycle took a slight detour to the 1970s, when Meatloaf's greatest hits began blaring through the complex. I can appreciate rock music like the rest of them, but at 7am on a Sunday? Even Mic Jagger has his limits. My plan is to introduce some David Guetta and Rihanna to my nostalgic neighbour who enjoys his blasts from the past, and then we'll be in business!

Day 5: I alighted at the matatu stage after coming home from work and decided to walk the rest of the way to my new flat instead of taking a second matatu. It's only a 20 minute walk, no biggie. But I forgot that in Mombasa in January, the hottest month of the year[7], 20 minutes is treacherous. Five minutes in, the beads of sweat began rolling down my forehead as I self-consciously wiped them away. Ten minutes in, I was drenched. By the fifteen minute mark, my clothes were stuck to me like latex and I was wondering what the heck I was doing walking in this heat. I scurried into my flat, turned the water pump on, stripped down, hopped into the shower, turned on the tap...and no water. I fiddled around for a bit (maybe you have to put your rear-end into everything here?) but no luck. There was not a drop of water coming from any of the taps in the flat. It took two repairmen, a ladder, a pair of pliers and two hours to get the H2O pumping through my pipes again. *Nashkuru.* My theory is that it was karma for my "If Moses can part an ocean, I can create one" incident on Day 3.

Day 6: Every day is a new day to learn something, and today I learned how to dispose of garbage. When I moved in, the first question I asked was "Is there AC?" followed by "What do I do with my garbage?" I really should have asked "Are there any Meatloaf fanatic neighbours who enjoy rocking out on Sunday mornings[8]?" Anyways, every person I asked responded "Your housemaid will take care of it." Upon hearing

---

[7] A.k.a. the month where sweat-rags are in every man's back-pocket and body odour coats the entire town

[8] Clearly I'm still a little bitter about my interrupted sleeping in day!

that I was housemaid-less, most people gasped, questioned why, asked if I was crazy, confirmed I was very brave and then said they had no idea where the garbage goes. And so I observed for a few days. One morning, I saw three plastic garbage bags outside my neighbour's house and when I returned home from work, they had magically disappeared. Aha! The next morning, I followed suit – I put my garbage outside my flat but much to my dismay, when I returned in the evening the bags were just as I had left them. Discreetly, I tried to bring the bags back up to my flat and re-strategize, but my cluck-clucking neighbour caught me red-handed. After confirming it was my garbage, she began a diatribe on the importance of cleanliness in the complex. I managed to sneak in two words ("no housemaid") and within seconds, she offered to have her housemaid collect my garbage along with hers every week. Things were definitely taking a turn for the better!

Day 7: Today, I got home from work with just enough time to squeeze in a quick yoga session (although supplanting yoga with a power nap might end up becoming routine by next week!), shower and go for prayers – which is located exactly 28 steps from my house. And before you mock me for my disproportionately large feet, you really ought to see just how close I live to *jamat khane*. I came back and grilled fresh tilapia – definitely a step up from peanut butter sandwiches. Unfortunately, somewhere between steaming vegetables and listening to *Allez! Olla! Ole!*[9], the water stopped running. Maybe it was God's way of telling me to take a break from doing the dishes? But not having water to take a shower the next morning...God, what was that all about?

Day 8: There's still no water and I am exhausted. It's tiring being a grown up and having to manage a new house. My quest to transform into a domesticated goddess is still very much in progress. After the adventures of this week, I take my hat off to all women out there balancing an Excel file in one hand and all-purpose cleaner in the other. You go girl!

---

[9] Youtube it. Really. Right now. Put this book down and shake what your mama gave you!

January 18, 2011

Toenails are so overrated

When I was a little girl, my dad used to take me to the horseracing track. We would sit for hours surveying horses pre-competition, picking the ones with the best odds[10] and root for our favourites til' the sun went down. Those hot summer days on the track taught me that in life, you win some and lose some, but at the end of the day, it's the experience that counts. Who cares if Ain't Misbehavin' beat Pumpernickel in the half mile race? Sorry Pumpernickel. It was the experience of sharing an adventure with my dad that made those afternoons so memorable.

There are a lot of things I have gained in my 5 months in Mombasa, my takings in this gamble. A new sense of independence, friendships that will last a lifetime and a whole new appreciation for the basic necessities in life are just a tip off the iceberg. There are a lot of things I've also lost through this experience – my preciseness with time (the slow pace of life here has definitely seeped into my veins), my desire to wear heels (flip flops are most certainly the way to go), my grasp of the English language (the more Swahili I learn, the more English I seem to lose)... and as of late, my big toenail.

---

[10] Or, I admit, the best names.

Every birthday since I was 10, my dream has been to grow. At 5'1" tall[11] I am probably the last person that belongs on a basketball court. And yet, there's something about the game that draws me in. The sound of a ball bouncing against a hardwood floor, the cacophony of sneakers pivoting on the court, the swish of a basketball through a net — these are the most satisfying sounds in existence. Moving to Africa where the only thing you do with a ball is kick it, I have most certainly experienced basketball-withdrawal symptoms. So when my pig-slaughtering, fisherman-saving neighbour casually mentioned his weekly pick-up game, I promptly invited myself to the next one. And so I went. Slightly terrified, and unsure of what to expect, I went.

I entered the gymnasium of the Aga Khan Academy and my heart sank — just picture, a group of six-feet tall, African men shooting hoops like they were gearing up for their next NBA game. And if it was a match up between the Toronto Raptors and them, my Shillings would definitely be put on these men. You can imagine, I surveyed the men, then looked critically at myself and wondered what the heck I was doing there. Alas, the feel of a basketball between my tiny fingers was too hard to pass up and so, I pretend-stretched[12] on the sidelines and finally entered the game....

Two and a half hours later, I was a dripping pool of sweat, but managed to bank a handful of baskets, impress a conglomerate of basketball superstars and agreed to be a weekly addition at their games. It was an unforgettable experience. Perhaps even more unforgettable was how my two big toes had swelled up and turned an unsightly shade of blue after the game. Two days later, I was hardly able to walk and was taken to the hospital, where the puzzled emergency doctor forcefully jammed a needle repeatedly through the nail bed to release the pressure. I cried in pain. I sincerely apologize to all my fellow Canadians for giving the impression that we are wooses with weird toes. My toenails remained blue for a few weeks (but hey, there's nothing a little nail polish can't fix) until a few days ago, when one nail popped off.

---

[11] ...and ¾

[12] I was actually giving myself a pep talk that maybe their warm-up had tired them out

For those of you who have stuck through my wide range of weird and wacky sports injuries[13], you will recall the toenail incident of 2009. Long story short: played in an inter-university sports tournament; 4 basketball games, 4 hockey games, 2 days; injured my toes and subsequently lost a toenail each in Malaysia, Singapore, Thailand and Indonesia while traveling that summer. 2011, add Kenya to the list. If past performance is any indicator of future success, as is the mantra of talent management, then Central Asia – I'm gunning for you...toenails and all!

---

[13] Thank you by the way!

February 2, 2011

Addictions

I am sitting in the courtyard of the Aga Khan Hospital over my lunch hour scrounging down fresh chips with masala spices — a house specialty! Laptop in hand, I had intended to document more tales of being a young Canadian almost-woman living on the other side of the world...housemaid-less.

But instead, a boy came along.

He couldn't have been more than five years old and had eyes larger than life. He ran from his parents who were sitting on a bench nearby, pulled up a chair beside me, managed to haul himself on top and just stared at me wide-eyed. I stuttered a mambo (the hipper version of a jambo) and he continued to stare and smile. Random side note: you know you're picking up a language when you dump your Lonely planet lingo for the real stuff. Supplant *jambo* with anyone of the following greetings: *mambo*, *sasa* or *vipi* and get a response of *poa!*, *fit!*, or my personal favourite, *fresh!* Swahili is such a gangster language sometimes.

Back to the boy. For twenty minutes, he pointed at objects around and asked *"He nini?"* — or, what's this? The table, the umbrella, the ketchup bottle, my sunglasses — this kid was relentless. And with every response, he gave a quick giggle and then moved to the next object, until his parents had to take him back inside the hospital.

Every once in while, life throws lessons your way in the most mysterious of forms. This one came in the shape of 3-foot tall pocket full of sunshine. In his utter quest for knowledge (or maybe more realistically, his fascination with Canadian accents), he reminded me to be curious.

The best part of moving a million miles away from home is that it heightens your sense of curiosity to the umpteenth degree. Everything is foreign and so, everything is something waiting to be explored. Road signs, newspapers even things as simple as what fruit is in season this month are opportunities for learning. Don't even get me started on grocery shopping in a new country — it's the single best thing about being oceans away!

I think that's what I love so much about traveling. When you've been bitten by the travel bug, it's really just a huge hit of curiosity. It's like an addiction. The more you learn, the more you realize how much you don't know. The more you experience, the more you realize you have left to experience. The more people you meet, the more you realize how many potential friends are out there just waiting to be met. The insatiable thirst to see new things and do new things consumes you — and the high that follows a new experience is impossible to describe. It's energizing. Traveling is like crack — it's a nightmare on your wallet, satisfying as heck and all it takes is one hit before you're hooked. The problem is when you stop. When you return back to your home, when the perils of reality hit and you realize you have school fees to pay off and a Prince to marry — a void of uncertainty that awaits me at the end of this incredible adventure. The thought of it scares me to pieces.

But alas, there's no good in analyzing the unknown. I'd much rather spend the time thoroughly savouring the last few bites of these masala chips. They really do make this world a better place.

February 10, 2011

People may just surprise you

I was sitting at a bar this past Saturday afternoon. This is a bar I've come to frequent quite regularly — partly because their passion juice is divine and partly because Francis the bartender encourages my feeble attempts at engaging in bar talk in Swahili[14]. But the real reason why I have a designated stool, why Francis knows my drink, why I choose to spend my weekends at the bar instead of the beach is because of a man named Bashir.

Bashir is an older fellow — how old, I have yet to figure out. His stories of his travels makes him seem like he's been around forever, but his clandestine conduct and cheeky sense of humour paint him as a man of much fewer years. We sit at the bar for hours discussing politics, education, sports. He swishes his drink in his glass, scans the room, clears his throat and then begins. He tells me about the export industry of Cadbury chocolates from South Africa and I tell him about our great Canadian beef. He tells me about the corruption in Kenya's government and I tell him about the long wait times in Canadian hospitals. He tells me about the effect of global warming on the African climate and I tell

---

[14] Bar talk is hard enough in English when you don't drink, let alone in another language

him about Canada's blistering winters. And somehow (usually after kicking back a few Tuskers), Bashir always sneaks in a remark about staying in Mombasa, for African men really know how to treat their women. I'm never quite sure what he means by this, but I don't dare ask – quite frankly, I'm not sure if I'm old enough to hear the details! At this bar, Francis supplies the drinks, Bashir supplies the conversation and Sky Sports supplies the football. It's a fabulous combination.

On Saturday, I arrived at the bar and found a group of older men fixated on the television with smiles stretching from ear to ear. Arsenal was up 3-0 against Newcastle, 10 minutes into the game. Even if the Magpies found a lucky leprechaun with a pot of gold, there was no way they could comeback from a 3-nil deficit. I made the mistake of saying this out loud[15], to which Bashir immediately responded by saying "My dear, never count someone out. People may just surprise you." Low and behold, eighty minutes later, Newcastle had scored 4 goals and drew the game 4-4. Bashir was right. Bashir is always right. He's like Confucius.

Fast forward 3 days. My work received a generous donation of toys from a donor in Dubai, and we were asked to find children's homes to distribute them to. I spent the morning at the Happy Rock Center in Likoni – an orphanage housing 27 children, established by a Dutch woman and her husband in 2005.

Here I met children who have suffered more than a lifetime's worth of sorrow in their short lives. Some were abandoned at hospitals while

---

[15] Apologies: I'm still perfecting this bar talk business

others watched their fathers use the family income to support a drinking addiction. The lucky few who have extended family were kicked out of their impoverished surroundings because an aunt's priority is to provide food and water to her own child before the child of her sister. Three children contracted the HIV/AIDS virus through breast milk and will have to incur the resulting hospital costs associated with a weakened immune system for the rest of their lives — they have no idea the cruelty and stigma that awaits them once they leave the home. These children should be counted out. They have no family, no assets, poor health and live in a country where opportunities aren't served on silver platters.

There is no reason not to count them out.

And yet, they have qualities you cannot put a price on — resilience, courage, humility. When I distributed toys to these kids, their faces lit up like they were the luckiest children in the world. They constructed their toy houses with determination, skill, resourcefulness and aptitude.

These children, however young, have learned to fend for themselves. Their circumstances have engrained in them the value of hard work and perseverance. These children should in every sense of the word be counted out. But I wouldn't do that just yet. As Bashir says, people have a tendency to surprise you. It's only the first half of their lives; they have a whole second half to show just what they are capable of. And I bet my Shillings that these kids are destined for greatness.

February 10, 2011

"Valentine's Day is not a real holiday"

Ili kwa kuweida kama leo. It was like any other day. But it shouldn't have been. It was Valentine's Day, and in my books, that's one special day. Sure, you can argue Valentine's is a capitalist ploy to generate revenue and stimulate the economy. Sure, it's a Hallmark invention which has spawned a cult known as 'antivalentinism' – people who attest the forced observation of romantic love due to societal pressures on a universally agreed-upon day is merely a breach of free will and therefore is not a reflection of true love. And sure, every couple in the world is celebrating on the exact same day – which completely undermines the definition of the word 'special'. Let alone, the blood pressure and overall stress inflicted upon the billions of attached men in the world likely escalates ten-fold on this single day alone. Theories aside, to me, Valentine's Day is about celebrating love – and love is the greatest force of all, even more so than gravity. Sorry Newton.

But alas, the day passed and not a mention was made of the V word. I did hear Enrique Iglesias play on my morning matatu ride, but Enrique plays quite often on these work commutes so awesome matatu music one: Valentine's zero. There was no sea of red across the town (strike

1), no couples frolicking the streets (strike 2), and worst of all, no cinnamon hearts (strike 3, batter's out). I love Mombasa to pieces and wouldn't change this experience for the world, but there are days when home can feel so very far away — and holidays have a tendency to bring those feelings to their peak.

In North America, when holidays aren't celebrated, you blame the recession. In Kenya, you blame *"mpango wa kando"*, literally "side plans." Get this, a side plan refers to an extra girlfriend a married man surreptitiously keeps on the side, in case Plan A goes awry. But when a man has a Plan B, C, and D all at the same time and one day to celebrate his love with all of them, you can see where things can get a bit problematic. Even a man who has mastered his time management skills would find himself needing more hours in the day. And in a place where the concept of savings is virtually unheard of, catering to the V-day needs of multiple side plans would do hefty damage to the poor chap's wallet. When I naively asked why he doesn't spend the day with his wife, his plan A, my colleague said casually that the man would not have any sideplans remaining after that day. Duh! The logic makes sense, but the outcome sucks for expats wanting to make it feel a little bit more like home.

Well, I guess if Mohammed can't go to the mountain, then you bring the mountain to Mohammed, or something like that. This was going to feel like Valentines Day, no matter how much chocolate I had to consume. I wore a little red dress, listened to sappy love songs all day long and wished every man, woman and child I met a Happy Valentine's Day, to which many responded "Valentine's is not a real holiday like Moi Day." Dually noted.

Valentine's Day in Africa may not be the traditional rose-giving, teddy bear-hugging, romantic comedy-watching type of holiday, but I suppose every day people in Mombasa express their care for one another. The way they thank God after you've said you slept well and awoke with peace. The way they spend what little money they have on food and share half of it with you. The way they open their hearts and make you feel at home, when real home is continents away.

I suppose 365 days of love trumps having it all condensed on one day — and, if you take into account 366 days of love during leap years, it really does cut out to be a good deal. But let it be known, next year I'm ordering myself a dozen roses and watching a marathon of chick-flicks...no matter what country I'm in[16].

---

[16] Update: I did celebrate Valentines Day 2012 with a dozen roses, but I didn't have to buy them for myself. I also was not able to watch a marathon of chick flicks as I was in meetings in Dar Es Salaam, Tanzania the whole day.

March 3, 2011

The day I figured out what I want to do when I'm all grown up

The sounds coming from the village were deafening. The screams of young children could be heard from miles away. They reverberated through the vast fields and were enough to send chills down your spine. Young infants were being poked and prodded in all directions. By the sounds of it, an extortion of catastrophic means could have been taking place behind the gates of this small primary school in Gwasheni village. But as you approached the mud walls of the school, it was a story of a much different tale.

The pokes were not acts of maliciousness, but rather the administration of immunizations that would help curb the unacceptably high under-five mortality rate in Coast Province. The children were being prodded to measure their weight, height and arm circumference — three indicators that can be triangulated to determine whether the child was malnourished. The sad part is that a majority of the children in this village were. Their screams understandably stemmed from their absolute fear of a health worker, for this was the first time many of these children had ever received medical attention.

…Rewind 5 hours…

It was 6 o'clock in the morning on a Saturday. Eyes barely open and half-asleep, I sauntered to the kitchen in desperate need of a jolt of caffeine. Today, I could not afford to be tired. I meticulously packed a bag of supplies, complete with hand sanitizer, bottles of water, and most importantly, loo roll. Today, loo roll would be my best friend. I put on a pair of sneakers (a rare occasion to wear closed shoes in Mombasa) and hopped into a tuk tuk off to work. Today, I was traveling to the most rural of the rural areas to bring basic health services to those who need it the most.

Alongside a few colleagues, we packed the pick-up truck with medical supplies, immunizations and medications, and began our journey. First stop: a small dispensary in the village of Muhaka. Here, we filled our empty bottles with gallons of water from a local stream, because where we were going, water is murky green in colour and worms are in plenty. We picked up local Community Health Workers and dispensary nurses, who squeezed themselves between medical supplies in the boot of the truck, and hit the road again. It was just past 8 o'clock in the morning and my caffeine boost had still not arrived. Where is Starbucks when you need it?

As we made our way along the winding dirt roads, crossing streams and herds of cows, it began to rain heavily. Downpours in Mombasa are a welcomed treat from the notorious heat, but when your open pick-up truck is filled with people and donated medical supplies, 'nashukuru' is not the first word on your mind. Our driver resourcefully created make-shift umbrellas with plastic bags and continued along. Time was of the essence – if we were on the road as the rains continued to pour down, the likelihood of our truck getting stuck in the mud was quite probable. A scary thought when you're in a sparsely populated place with no network connection, limited fuel and open to a known community of roaming elephants.

We managed to arrive at the primary school of Gwasheni village just as the rains stopped and the sun peaked out through clouds. Nashukuru. It was 10 o'clock in the morning and already, there was a crowd of women and children waiting for us. We quickly surveyed the school, organized supplies, removed dirt and spiders from each classroom with tree branches and began taking clients. For the next 5 hours, it was a non-stop marathon of playing House.

I began the day in the HIV/AIDS testing centre, where according to Kenyan law, every person must know their HIV status. I pricked the fingers of over 300 men, women and children over the age of 12, drew blood onto testing strips, cleaned the wound, wiped away tears in some cases, analyzed test results and informed them of their status. Every time I said "Hakuna HIV", the smiles that lit up their faces made me smile just as much. Every time. And in cases with a positive test strip, I referred them to the Community Nurse who ran a more comprehensive test. When HIV supplies ran out, I had to announce in my very broken Swahili that more testing equipment was on its way. My message was received by a classroom full of laughs and I was called 'mzungu' or white person, the rest of the day.

I then moved onto registration, where every community member's details were taken down before seeing a nurse. Here, I met an elderly lady, who when asked for her age, declared proudly she was somewhere between eighty and a hundred years old. We settled for eighty-two. I offered to assist her walk to the treatment area. Though her bones were weak and her skin was adorned with the wrinkles of time, she walked by herself with her back as straight as an arrow. I commented on how strong of a woman she must be and was told that she had walked for miles from her homestead to the school just to see a doctor. Humbling does not even begin to describe it.

I next moved onto the growth monitoring area where every child was weighed and measured to check for malnourishment. It was here that the cries of children being prodded and poked could be heard from miles away.

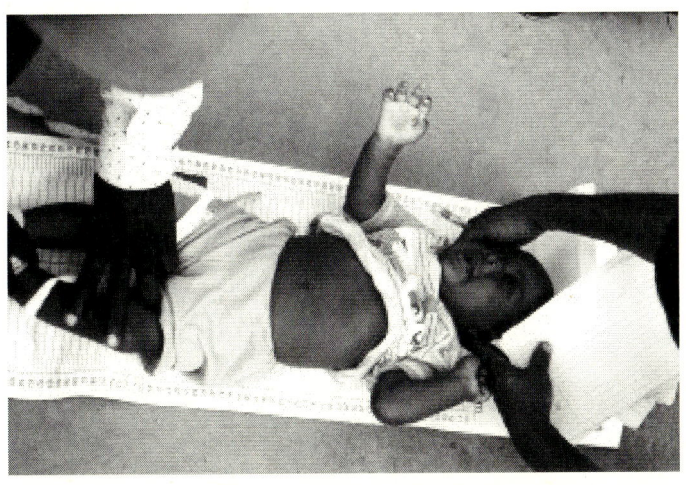

And so I sang. I picked up the children who had come on the backs of their elder siblings and sang to them "Twinkle Twinkle Little Star", "Row Row Row Your Boat" and by popular demand, "Waka Waka Africa". Lesson learned: when a child is upset, 'waka waka' are your two favourite words.

It was mid-afternoon by now. I ventured to the consultation and treatment area and observed a community nurse see patient after patient. Her knack for communicating was commendable. In a village as remote as Gwasheni, even Swahili cannot get you very far. Tribal languages are common speak — but which of the seven languages to use depends entirely on the family lineage of the individual. This nurse tactfully manoeuvred through all communication barriers and treated each client in an efficient manner. The most common ailment was open sores on the scalp and skin caused by ringworms, which are contracted through dirty water or through the soles of the feet. And in rural villages where shoes are luxurious commodities and many children walk on open defecated areas, worms are easy to pick up.

As I was leaving the treatment area, a young woman grabbed my hand and pleaded in a language I did not understand. I tried exhaustively to make sense of what she was saying, and barely managed to get that she wanted to skip the queue of over a hundred people and see the nurse right away. I told this to the nurse who treated her and her children quickly and sent them off. Later, I found out that this 21-year old woman had brought with her ten children — four of whom were hers, the remaining were the children of her husband's other wives. As the youngest wife, she was tasked with the responsibility of bringing all the children of the household to see a nurse. She was desperate to get back home to make dinner for the entire family before her husband returned from work. This was a woman younger than me whose cries told the story of absolute fear and exhaustion. It was heartbreaking.

I finished the day in the pharmacy where I assisted in dispensing drugs and distributing porridge to all children deemed malnourished. Though it was hot, you forgot that you were tired. You forgot that you hadn't eaten all day. You forgot that it was a Saturday. All those things seemed irrelevant in that moment. Being amongst people whose first experience with a health professional had come at the age of 82;

people who had smiles beaming from ear to ear because they received free Ibuprofen; little boys who had carried their baby brothers on their backs for miles; it certainly makes you step back and put life into perspective.

I wish I could say that we left the village and everyone lived happily ever after. But the truth is development work has a darker shade often hidden from stakeholders' reports and the media. As we were wrapping up supplies, health workers and nurses openly pocketed the remaining donated medications for personal usage. Though they were servicing hundreds of poor community members, they themselves have minimal incomes and limited access to affordable drugs. Other health workers took bags of porridge for their own family, so when a group of children arrived at the school, there was only one bag of porridge remaining to distribute amongst the lot of them. There were challenges in confirming the validity of people's testimonials of their symptoms. Many claim to have headaches so that they can receive free antibiotics and subsequently, trade those drugs in the village for food. But can you blame a starving man who trades what's given to him for something more meaningful? It's pretty darn creative, in fact.

We spent an entire day giving medical attention to people who are too poor or live too far away to access care from local dispensaries. We slaved away at ensuring every child's measurements were taken, every woman was counselled on family planning methods, every person was instructed on proper use of medications given. And yet, we reached only four hundred of the thousands of community members in Gwasheni. The simple question to ask is, 'why not do this every day until every single person has been attended to?' Two reasons: #1 Community outreaches such as this are financially demanding. Our partners, Tsavo Power, only fund a limited number of outreach days per year to meet their corporate responsibility quota. #2 Outreach days are not sustainable sources of development. Sure, we may have treated hundreds of children for ringworms, but if they continue to consume dirty water and play in open defecation zones, then really all we're providing is a band-aid solution. It would be more prudent to invest the money in finding sustainable sources of clean water.

My placement at the Community Health Department has exposed me to the potential of doing incredibly rewarding work. But it has equally shown me the struggles and gaps in development work that can pose as real challenges. Now more than ever, I have an overwhelming desire to dedicate my life to understanding and bridging those gaps, so that every person around the world has access to quality medical services.

March 29, 2011

Ode to the Matatu Driver

Dear Mr. Matatu Man,

    I wait for you longingly
    Along the side of the road.
    For minutes or sometimes longer
    With my heavy workbag load.

    You operate without a schedule,
    And have trouble keeping time.
    As I wait, I curse with malice
    Words unrepeatable in this rhyme.

    But then I hear your music
    Reverberate through the streets
    And you wisp me off to work
    To the sound of bongo beats.

    I manoeuvre my way through your van
    To find an empty seat
    And open the window to catch a breeze
    A relief from the Mombasa heat.

You swerve your way through traffic
And honk along the way.
I sit at the back petrified.
And pull out my tasbih to pray.

You nearly miss a blind man,
And skim the surface of a truck.
We approach a queue of cars
And in traffic you are stuck.

But no.

Traffic is not a concept
Found within your head.
We hop the curb, cut the queue
And take a side street instead.

Your van may have its issues
No mirrors and no lights
But what it lacks in mechanics
It more than makes up for in sights.

Because from your matatu window, I see...

Markets full of used clothing,
Shoes, row upon row.
For in the absence of shopping malls
Second hand is the way to go.

I see men carrying barrels of water
Sweat rolling down their backs.
While goats graze by the side of the road,
With herds of cows behind their tracks.

I see mama's strolling through town
Balancing buckets on their head
A baby on the side, one on the back
And one in front being fed.

I see little girls sing joyfully
As their mothers braid their hair.

While children hop from car to car
Begging for change to spare.

I see women laying on the ground
Five babies by their side.
Their pain and anguish of being homeless
Are emotions too poignant to hide.

As I survey the world around me,
And take in the sights of the day.
It is clear that everything I know
Is millions of miles away.

And yet, there is something captivating
A force that draws me near.
It fills me with curiosity
And diminishes all my fear.

The more I learn about this country
Through every bend, twist and curve
The more inequality I come to see
The greater my desire to serve.

Although your matatu is a death sentence
Any day it could fall apart.
It's shown me the real Mombasa
The place where I have lost my heart…

Sincerely, your loyal rider,
Sabrina

May 20, 2011

It's raining, it's pouring...

My feet were soaking wet; my toes covered in mud. My meticulously straightened hair lay curly and damp on my shoulders, already beginning to frizz. Just as I was approaching the gates of my work, a tuk tuk raced by, splashing puddles of water across my newly washed dress pants. Pants that were just two days ago, soaked in a bucket of soapy water, scrubbed with a plastic brush, rinsed in a second bucket of water and secured with clothespins on the line by my balcony to dry — a process I've become accustomed to calling laundry.

Torrential downpours have become commonplace in the last few weeks. Although they are a welcomed treat from the scorching Mombasa heat, they often bring life to a standstill. With darkened skies and heavy rainfalls, power outages are almost always next to follow suit. Unless you are one of the lucky few able to afford a generator, no power means no lights, no fans and more times than not, no network connection. All that can be heard is the faint buzzing of mosquitoes, as they bask in their new water-filled playground. Street vendors close up shop, fresh mahamris are tucked away under sheets of plastic and women dressed in brightly-coloured kangas haphazardly cover their back-ridden children with loose material and disappear out of sight. When it rains in Mombasa, life seems to stop.

And when the rains finally subside and the sun begins to peak through the clouds, the air fills with a humidity that envelopes your body and fills your lungs with the sharp stench of sweat and sewage. It leaves you in an even more vegetative state, left completely incapacitated by the whims of Mother Nature.

As I approached the metal gates of my office, muddy toes and all, I glanced over at Cleopus, the fruit man outside the hospital, to say hello – one of my favourite morning rituals. But for the first time, he didn't wave back. He didn't hear me. He was lost in his own world singing away as he rearranged papayas with impeccable style, treating each fruit as if it were a piece of art work – a precious gem not to be taken for granted. Fruits are his life, his joy. I approached Cleopus and wished him a good morning to which he put his hand across his heart and said "salaama, salaama", as he does every morning. But in the nine months that I've known him, never had I seen him so overjoyed. Never had I seen his pearly whites shine as bright as they did that day. When I asked him why, he simply answered "Mvua mingi" or 'lots of rain'. Lots of rain? The same rain that had proven a worthy match to my waterproof mascara? The same rain that turned the streets into a puddle-filled obstacle course? The same rain that took inefficiency to a whole new level?

What I learned was the same rain that I had come to dislike with a passion also left the soil rich and well-nourished, making it ideal for crop growth. With farms prospering, Cleopus had access to a greater variety of fruits at a cheaper cost. Ultimately, more customers, more profits and more money to look after his children. Downpours are indeed a cause worth celebrating when the final beneficiaries are hungry children. During heavy rainfalls, many families spend the night hoisting buckets across the house to collect the rainwater. On a good night, the water collected is enough to sustain a family for a week. That means in urban communities, less money spent on water consumption and in rural villages, less time required to collect daily water from the community pump. Most often, it is the women and young girls of the household tasked with the responsibility of making the long, treacherous journey to fetch water. The time young girls spend balancing heavy loads of water on their heads, can be more valuably spent in school. Worst still, empty isolated roads are not the safest places for women of any age. A week's worth of rain water, although small in amount, can keep girls focused on their studies for just a few extra hours a day, and can give elder women some much deserved rest.

As I walked away from Cleopus' fruit stand towards my office, I looked back at the greying skies and flooded streets and smiled. No longer was the rain something to be cursed; rather a blessing to be grateful for. Rain showers are a symbol of growth in a country where protecting the environment has become secondary to capital gain. The rains provide hope to people like Cleopus, that in spite of the rampant corruption and rising cost of living, every person can wake up each morning and have something worth singing about. And hope is a very powerful thing.

June 16, 2011

Just have faith

After living in Africa for nearly a year, there are very few things that phase me. Even without electricity, air conditioning and running water, life always seems to sort itself out. Just like Robert Frost said "In three words, I can sum up everything I've learned about life: it goes on." I suppose Frost's mantra works well and fine in North America — but bring it to Kenya, and its foundation begins to shake. Let me tell you about my Friday night.

For weeks, I have been anticipating my homecoming to Mombasa — the sanctuary I left four weeks ago in exchange for the chaos and madness of Nairobi. Although I am coming to appreciate the idiosyncrasies of city life, my heart still longs for the home-feel of Mombasa; and my stomach aches for the Coast's nyama choma and madafu. Three weeks ago, I booked my ticket back and have been counting down the days ever since. The excitement of basking in the heat again coupled with attending a close friend's graduation and a special birthday celebration had claimed a rightful X on my calendar.

Last Friday was the big day. I barely managed to compose myself during meetings — even with budgetary constraints and delays in new projects, I had a smile permanently plastered to my face. And rightfully so, because I was going home. The cab driver was arranged, the bags were packed — everything had been accounted for. Everything except the infamous Nairobi jams.

Although leaving hours before my flight, we found ourselves in the middle of a traffic crisis. My driver, Charles, resourcefully hopped curbs and trekked along every side street possible but in every direction we turned, there were a queue of cars. And so we waited. In an impassable jam of cars, we waited. As the clock ticked, etching closer and closer to my 9pm flight departure, we waited. It was 7:32pm, and we had only managed to make it inches away from my house. I desperately asked Charles if I would make the flight to which he answered "No problem, madam, we will make it." I appreciated his optimism.

As we waited, the most interesting things started to happen. People turned off their engines, stepped out of their cars and began intellectual conversations with neighbouring strandees on politics and the economy. Others rolled down their windows and began bickering in Swahili about the best way to get out of this mess. It was a demonstration of a sense of community in its finest form. With my flight departing in less than an hour, I did not give my driver the luxury of catching some shut eye — as many of the drivers beside us did, as they waited for the traffic to clear. Instead, we daringly reversed onto oncoming traffic, turned around and raced down another side street, only to find a queue of matatus.

Although traffic has an incredible ability of creating an identity around a shared experience, it was here that I learned its equally impressive ability to open the doors to darker sides of society. We may see it as a nuisance and waste of time, but street boys see traffic as an opportune moment to fill their pockets. On that night, I witnessed two robberies steps away from my cab. One where a cell phone was taken out of the hands of a person sitting in a matatu and the other, a briefcase stolen from an expat who jumped out of his car and ran after the thief yelling 'catch him, catch him', but it was too late. Not only was I late for a flight, was miles away from the airport and had a dying cell phone battery, I was also concerned about our safety. I ventured to ask

Charles again if we were okay and he said again in his most reassuring voice, "No problem, madam, we'll make it."

Three hours later, we were still stuck in traffic and had been grazed by a lorry who daringly hopped a curb but underestimated the amount of space available. Thankfully, there was no damage done to our car; just a knocked-off side mirror to which I rolled down the window quickly, arranged the mirror back in place, and rolled the window back up. It was now well past 9pm. I had missed my flight, but heard there was one more flight to Mombasa that night at 11pm. As I took a deep breath and felt a sense of hope again, I looked at the dashboard only to see we were low on fuel. I watched the line anxiously the rest of the way as it inched closer and closer towards Empty, willing it to reverse directions towards the Full, until finally the yellow light switched on. That darn yellow light indicating our fuel supply had drained completely. I asked Charles in my most pleading voice if we were okay to which he responded "Now, madam, we have a problem."

A missed flight, luring street boys, no phone battery, a suitcase full of my best belongings, my DSLR camera, laptop, blackberry and passport all in hand and now, no fuel. Life was not looking so good.

I am not sure how it happened, or why it happened, but somehow as Charles turned onto a side street to re-strategize, there at the end of the road, we saw the light. It was a brightly lit petrol station beckoning us towards it. With no fuel left, we managed to put the car on neutral and roll down the road until we came close enough to the station to fill up. Nashukuru sana. Now that our tank was full of fuel, our hearts were full of thanks and the roads were beginning to clear up, we swerved our way in and out of lanes and made it to the airport. What should have been a half an hour ride took four hours, but we made it.

I waltzed to the Kenya Airways ticket counter, described my taxing journey to get there and asked to be put on the 11pm flight, only to find out it was full. And the next flight was departing at 6am the following morning. I tried everything — even asking if there was space in the cockpit — but alas, my luck had run dry. I was put on a wait list but was told it would be more prudent to go home, get some rest and come back the next morning.

I sat by the ticket counter, deflated and nearly in tears. All I wanted was to go home. And then...10 minutes before the flight was to leave, by some miracle, one seat opened up. I was so happy, I hugged the sales agent. I raced down the security check, across the runway and sank into my seat just seconds before we took off. I landed in Mombasa safe and sound later that night and had the most incredible weekend at home.

P.S. After arriving back to Nairobi on Monday morning, I was looking at pictures and reminiscing about the weekend until I was interrupted by the most horrible sound. It sounded like something was choking, or dying, or both. And then, I saw smoke coming from the hood of my cab. The cab made a few more valiant efforts but died shortly after, in the middle of the road. Thankfully a few men on the street helped us push the cab off the road, but soon after got into a heated argument with the driver about getting some money in exchange for their efforts. I managed to get into another cab and reached work just in time for a few meetings.

So maybe Robert Frost wasn't so wrong after all. Life does go on. But I think after my weekend mishaps, my mantra will forever be: Just have faith.

August 8, 2011

One year ago

One year ago, I sat in the Amsterdam airport, hours away from beginning an 8-month journey in Kenya through the Aga Khan Foundation Canada - International Development Management Fellowship programme. I was anxious, I was scared, and I was excited by the possibilities. One year ago, I was sitting in the Amsterdam airport reading the introductory sections of my Swahili book, frantically trying to memorize the hellos and goodbyes of the seemingly foreign language. One year ago, I was a young, naive girl wanting to make a difference in the world.

Today, I sit in the Amsterdam airport, waiting to board a flight back home to Toronto. My legs are scarred with mosquito bites and my clothes are tattered from not seeing a washing machine and dryer for a year. Today, I sit in the Amsterdam airport overwhelmed by the efficiency of the check-in process, astonished by the cleanliness of the loos and blinded by row upon row of Cosmopolitan magazines in the airport bookshop. Today, I am a strong, independent woman who has fallen in love with a country millions of miles away.

When I began this adventure in East Africa, I was expecting to learn about best case practices in community health and proposal development. My goal was to become a Master of monitoring and evaluation and a Lord of logical framework analyses. I was hoping to have the experience of a lifetime and be anxious to return back to Canada after 8 months (to what I thought was the 'real world'), perhaps a little smarter and slightly more tanned.

Never did I expect to stay a year, or have a return ticket back to Kenya in 3 weeks time.

Everyone describes their stint after University abroad as life-changing, myself included at times. But what I've learned is that life-changing is just an easy way of veiling the tough, raw emotions entangled in the experience. It was scary waiting in long queues at the hospital for test results confirming I had contracted a parasite while working in the field. It was heart-breaking spending my weekends with HIV-positive orphans knowing the kind of stigma and barriers that awaited them. It was lonely celebrating my birthday in bed with malaria. It was discouraging having patrons bribe the store clerk at a local printing shop to have their documents printed first when I and others had waited patiently in line for our turn. It was uncomfortable being in community meetings and sit across from men with wandering eyes and albeit, not the best of intentions. It was demoralizing to see an orphanage covet for money and toys and not see any of it reach the children. It was terrifying having a friend robbed in broad daylight while walking together to the market, and frustrating watching the police officers beat the thief with their AK-47s later that day at the police station. At times, I just wanted to click my heels and come home.

But... The loneliness instantly disappeared when spending evenings at zumba classes with new work-out buddies, dancing the Saturday nights away at beach bars and cheering on my boys on Sundays with fellow Liverpool fans. The frustration was trumped by seeing the tears of joy of a mother who had safely delivered her baby at a health centre, when she had previously lost her other children in home deliveries. The scariness was forgotten when I was jamming to Bongo flavour on my morning matatu ride to work. The discouragement was superseded by complete satisfaction when I was sipping fresh passion juice and madafu for a fraction of the price of a Tim Hortons' coffee. And the discomfort was quickly supplanted by a sense of accomplishment after bargaining down the price of vegetables at the local market in Swahili.

Although I brushed up on my monitoring and evaluation skills and contributed to a number of grant proposals during my year abroad, it was the things I learned outside the office that really made their mark. I learned how to navigate through the idiosyncrasies of working in the laid-back Coast, where productivity and to-do lists are rendered unworthy components against the heat. I learned how to look absolutely confident walking down the streets of Nairobi, even if I had no idea where I was going. I learned the art of dressing and putting on make-up in the dark when the electricity cut out, as it often did. When I left for this adventure, never did I expect to rock a one-week old baby in my arms under a mango tree outside a village dispensary in Kwale. Never did I expect to become the proud mother of a baby elephant named Kainuk. Never did I expect to have my understanding of the world be completely questioned when exposed to the deficiencies and unfairness of the primary health care system in rural communities. Never did I expect to fall in love.

I thought I was going to Africa to leave my footprint. Little did I know that Africa was going to leave an even bigger footprint on me. This experience has transformed me; it has challenged me; it has enriched me. For the next three weeks, I plan to thoroughly enjoy McDonalds, bagels with cream cheese, and driving on the right side of the road. And then, back to Nairobi I go for another year to continue this incredible journey – for there are more mango trees to climb, matatus to ride, people to meet, and lessons to learn. *Kwaheri.*

November 8, 2011

The genetic lottery

My name is Sabrina Natasha Premji and I am a lottery winner. The genetic lottery, that is. I am a 23-year old woman born and raised in Toronto, Canada. I grew up playing t-ball in a recreational league and going to pottery classes after school. I have had access to good quality education and health care services. My life has been inculcated with reality television, Facebook status updates and fast food chains. Safety, security, and stability — these are not words that have ever crossed my mind because in my world, they are a given. I am educated, I am independent, I am empowered.

But my winning ticket in this genetic lottery could have easily been given to someone else. And my story could have been written much differently.

I could have been born in a rural East African community at the hands of a traditional birth attendant — an unskilled, untrained woman who would be paid in kind or the equivalent of a few dollars to deliver me. Unskilled deliveries outside health facilities are a reality faced by approximately 50-60% of women in sub-Saharan Africa — often because of the unavailability of transport to reach a health centre, the lack of funds to support a skilled delivery, or a cultural belief of appearing as a coward within the community for seeking medical services. My umbilical cord could have been cut by a used razor, greatly increasing the risk of infection. If my mother did not survive – as every minute, a woman dies during labour or delivery primarily due to postpartum hemorrhage, eclampsia, obstructed labour and sepsis – I would be without breast milk, a crucial element to the development of a healthy immune system and likely be amongst the 3.5 million children worldwide that die of diarrhea, malaria, malnutrition or other treatable diseases each year before their 5th birthday.

Assuming I am still alive and my family is able to afford school fees, I have the privilege of walking kilometers each morning to attend school. It is here that I am exposed for the first time to a world of possibility – of reading and writing, of learning English, of making something of my life. I dream of being a teacher. However, in spite of being motivated and working hard every day to excel at my studies, my marks fall short to those of my male classmates. Why? Because I miss one week of school each month during my menstrual cycle. Since I do not have access to sanitary napkins – a yearly supply of sanitary napkins to keep one girl in school costs about $30 – and the school I attend does not have running water or pit latrines, it is nearly impossible to attend classes during days of menstruation. My absenteeism is noticed and I join the other 87% of girls in East African communities who do not complete primary school.

Uneducated and unskilled, I spend my days assisting in household chores and helping raise my younger siblings. I am soon married to a man who is twice my senior and shortly thereafter, contract HIV/AIDS. The prevalence of condoms has increased dramatically in sub-Saharan Africa however, it is commonly seen as a method of preventing HIV/AIDS and not as a form of contraception, resulting in 50% of new HIV/AIDS infections occurring within marriage or cohabiting couples – a statistic further propagated by 11% of men and 2% of women in sub-Saharan Africa reporting extramarital partners. For months, I live my life as a nobody – a stranger to the world, a stranger to myself. I have no identity, no status, no national ID card – I am not seen as a person until I give birth to my first child. I give birth to a child almost every year in the years to follow – partly because of limited knowledge around family planning methodologies, partly because of fear of refusing my husband and partly because if some of my children die of disease, I will have other children who can support me as I age.

To the outside world, I am perceived as a passive spectator; a coward who does not take ownership of her life. But how can I, when every day I am worried my children may fall sick and I will not have the financial resources to care for them? How can I, when my community is struck by drought year upon year and cannot harvest enough crops to make a living? How can I, when I fear for my daughter's safety as she walks for miles to fetch our daily water from the community water pump? I am constantly living in survival mode. Every day is a struggle. My life comes to an end at the tender age of 55, and I can only hope that my children may be blessed with the opportunity to craft a better life for themselves than I could.

My name is Sabrina Natasha Premji and I have won the lottery — but the problem is, I am a winner in a game I don't want to play. Because this isn't a game, this is life. My takings — good education, access to quality health care, food security — should not be winnings to the lucky few. Disparities in economic opportunity, death due to preventable diseases, uneducated women because of lack of sanitary napkins — these are realities that are unacceptable in an age when the Kardashians gross US$65 million a year.

Too often, we turn away from these harsh realities because it is easier not to look, it is easier not to care — because once we begin to care, it becomes our problem. When we accept it as our problem, we often feel helpless because the injustice of the world seems beyond our reach, Our challenge is to throw ourselves into the middle of it all — to internalize the situation as much as possible and seek to understand its complexity; to allow ourselves to feel a visceral reaction to stories of others without becoming paralyzed by the emotion; to contextualize the issues from a grassroots perspective while equally being able to step back far enough from the situation to understand how to solve it; and to use the innovation and technology that all too often we take for granted to engage and empower communities to develop locally-based, sustainable solutions. I suppose I am a so-called winner of the genetic lottery but what matters most is what I choose to do with those winnings. I choose to make a difference.

November 15, 2011

Authenticity

We all have flaws. Small imperfections built into our design plan. They tend to teach us something, or help us grow in some way — and for the most part, are innocuous by nature. But we also all have the flaw, that one glitch in our DNA that holds us back from becoming the people we are meant to become. Shakespeare described this as a tragic flaw, pointing to Hamlet's inability to act and MacBeth's ambition as the cause of their demise.

If Shakespeare had told my tale, I always thought he would point to my inability to iron as my tragic flaw. Definitely an image-compromiser and a relationship-breaker. It is only after leaving the capitalist woes and materialist urges of North America that I realize my tragic flaw has always been my desire to fit in. Unconsciously or not, every choice I have made — where to shop, what movie to watch, which radio station to listen to — has been influenced by an unrelenting craving to find a sense of belonging. In many ways, I have had to — because I have grown up in a society where admitting to having not seen Avatar is considered to be blasphemous and not having a Facebook account is simply unforgivable. We are unquestionably influenced by our peers. Research shows that we are exhibiting an unparalleled distrust of governments and institutions and tend to make decisions based on what our friends are doing or people we choose to trust. But if you take influence one step further and make decisions, often unknowingly, to find a sense of belonging amongst others to be able to fit in better, that's when life becomes tricky... and voila, my tragic flaw.

And then I came to Africa. A place where my skin colour is ten shades lighter than my fellow matatu-commuters and my ability to deal with the scorching heat of the Coast puts the community to shame.

Working on primary health care initiatives in rural communities, I spend many of my days in areas far removed from the chaos of cars and distraction of poorly dubbed Mexican soap operas. I do not fit in by any means. I walk through villages to the sounds of children yelling '*mzungu!*' or 'white person!' — children who are bewildered by the colour of my skin and the feel of my hair. I engage with women whose life experiences could not be any more dissimilar to mine and play with their babies whose upbringing does not bare any resemblance to the playgrounds and Sesame Street characters of my childhood. And yet, in spite of the marked differences in appearance, in attitudes, in goals, it is here in the field that I feel a genuine sense of belonging. Sitting in a thatch-roofed hut, eating beans and chapatti with hands, I forget about our differences or our lives being oceans apart — at the end of the day, we are people lost in a conversation about the joys of football or the perils of drought. The field has a magical way of stripping down the clutter and noise of this world down to its simplest elements and creating an enabling environment for conversation and connection.

My work in East Africa has shown me that maybe we all try too hard to fit in. We perceive superficial, materialistic commodities as entry tickets into a world where we can all relate to one another and feel a sense of belonging, only to forget about connecting with people on a much more fundamental level. When you shift your focus from what you have to what you feel, you will find connections in the most unlikely of places — because at the end of the day, we are all linked together by core human emotions. Common threads of hope and love, of longing and loss, of pain and sadness.

A mama who spends her days rearing chickens to pay her children's school fees in a rural East African village is no different than a stiletto-borne woman on a Blackberry in New York City who sends her children to a private school on the Upper East Side. Both women are connected by a relentless desire to provide the best for their children. Young African boys playing football with a ball made out of scraps on a dusty makeshift field without shoes are no different than a group of children playing house league soccer on a well-manicured pitch in London. There is a sense of absolute joy and energy – and a need to play – that unites these children, no matter how far apart their worlds may be. A young *toto* strapped to the back of his mother with a kanga as she walks to fetch water is no different than a baby sauntering through the streets of Queen West in his stroller. Both are curiously taking in their surroundings, developing notions of the world they will soon grow up in.

There is immense value in the plurality of thoughts and peoples. But there is also something to be said about finding commonalities, shared points of connection amongst people who on the surface, could not be more unlike one another. I have learned that no matter how many hours I spend practicing my Kiswahili or how many *kangas* I wear, it is impossible to not stand out in a rural Kenyan community. But for the first time in my life, instead of hiding behind the shadows or trying to blend in, I seek to embrace the difference. No longer do I wish to fit in – instead I wish to connect with people at a more basic, fundamental level because this is where trust develops, where ideas begin to flourish and where community development should lay its roots.

November 30, 2011

Silence

I walked through the winding alleyways of the slum, my eyes focused on the ground below me. I tried nervously to avoid slipping into piles of mud and animal waste, created by a heavy rainfall the previous night. I had received a briefing during the one-hour car ride from the city to the Mlolongo slums – and yet, as I inched closer and closer to the entrance of the small house, the theory, the problem analysis, the context seemed to take a backseat to the sinking feeling in my stomach. I removed my shoes at the gate and was welcomed into the dark room, pungently marked by the smell of urine and feces. There in front of me, were two dozen children – some sitting on a broken couch, many lying on the ground eerily still. My presence did not phase them; their eyes remained fixated on the bare walls and low ceilings of the small room. These children were hollow – their perfect little bodies remained still, safe for their rising bellies with each breath, but it was clear that their minds and hearts were worlds away. A small, confined space with more than twenty babies – and all I could hear was silence.

Slum settlements have become a reality for millions of Kenyans who have left their rural homes for the promise of work in the big city, only to be hit with burgeoning food prices and lack of employment opportunities. Often, women have to travel long distances outside of the slum to find work, or are forced into prostitution to make ends meet. The problem is while these women slave away at making a living, their children are left alone during the day to fend for themselves.

Call it innovation, call it an act of kindness, call it entrepreneurship – many women in the slum community have opened 'baby care centres' to look after these children – a makeshift daycare concept, if you will. For less than a dollar a day, mothers can bring their children to these centres and ensure they are watched over from dawn to dusk. If being observed was the only pressing need, these centres would more than suffice. But babies need more than that. They need food – sometimes provided by the baby care centre, sometimes provided by the mother, many times forgotten, or unaffordable, by both. Young children need love, they need a sense of belonging for emotional development, according to early childhood development principles. However, with many baby care centres serviced by only one person, caregiver attachment is an unlikely phenomenon. Babies need movement, they need physical activity to develop an understanding of what things feel like. Being placed on their backs for most of the day, many of these children do not build the muscle strength in their lower body, resulting in four and five-year olds being unable to walk. Many of the children in these centres exhibited delays in cognitive development due to a lack of stimulation. A majority of the children were stunted for growth. All were at risk every moment of the day of contracting an infectious disease.

As I made my way through the various centres, it took every effort to hold back a waterfall of tears. It took every ounce of courage to converse with the owners of the daycares in my most friendly Kiswahili, applauding them for their efforts. Every part of me wanted to scream out. What struck me the most was in that 10ft x10ft room, the duality of an unfair, cruel world was contrasted by the very innocence contained within that space. Children who knew no world other than this one. Children whose lives could have been completely different if their seeds were simply planted in a different soil.

As international development practitioners, it is our job to design programs and identify funds to better the lives of poor. But as human beings, it is our **responsibility** to do what is within our power to create environments of opportunity for all, including those of the children in the Mlolongo slums. Whether it be through advocacy, policy development or resource mobilization, each of us has a role to play in equalizing the playing field. Each of us has a role to play in making this world a better place.

December 24, 2011

Moments

A moment. It is the smallest possible denominator in life. We plan our lives in years, we set goals based on months, we have to-do lists by the day, but everything eventually comes down to the moment. Life is an endless string of moments and I have a tendency to get swept away in them. For that single instant, to be completely bewitched by living, breathing, feeling the splendor of a moment — it truly is a beautiful thing. I look back at nights sitting on the beach in Diani gazing up at a spectacle of stars; I recall long drives on winding roads towards unchartered lands to watch a thundershower over the Rift Valley; I can close my eyes and remember fondly stopping on the side of the road near a farm to bite into a succulent Malindi papaya before it reached the city market. I could fall back in these moments again in a heartbeat because they bare the possibility of a lifetime of happiness. And at the end of the day, that's what we all crave. An eternity of happiness.

But what happens when the moment is not one of happiness, but of heartbreak? What happens when that single second evokes so much emotion that we get lost in the moment — where the lines of reality and fantasy become so burred, that it is impossible to find our way out? I have faced that fear every single day for the last year and a half living in East Africa — not knowing if today is the day that the pain will be too great, the stories of life and death will be too overwhelming, the disparities in quality of life will be too disheartening that I will lose myself in the field and not be able to find my way out. There are days when I feel paralyzed. I feel like the solutions are beyond me, are beyond us all. I feel like what I have to offer pales in comparison to the magnitude of the problem. In those moments, I pray for a hand to hold me, for a voice to comfort me, to guide me out of the moment and back to a place where I can do something about it. A place where my head rules my heart.

But maybe the heartache is part of a masterfully crafted plan to facilitate action. An unmotivated head is worthless until it is combined with an unrelenting passion to drive it — and what better motivator than pain. There is so much pain in this world. So much pain. I have borne witness to only a fraction of it and even that has been enough to unnerve me. I can close my eyes and picture babies in an urban slum outside of Nairobi being tied and locked in confined spaces while their mothers seek work for the day. With no stimulation and no engagement from a caregiver, they tend to grow up with physical and developmental delays, thereby hindering their chances of thriving in an already disabling environment. Images like that haunt me, but also motivate me to step up to the plate and do something about it. They invite kindness and humility but equally, summon the ability to think critically and strategically — a perfect marriage between the heart and the head.

I can close my eyes and imagine the man who finds shelter near the matatu stand by my flat in Nairobi. His feet are bare, as he paces back and forth mindlessly by the side of the road. His hair is in disarray — likely not having been washed or shaved in months. His body is filthy and his pants drape past his waist, weighed down by the empty soda bottles he ties to his make-shift rope belt. His mind is not here. It is clear this fellow is suffering from serious psychological distress; one amongst a growing number of people who can no longer afford the rising cost of living in Kenya. My heart bleeds for him while my head ponders his options for seeking help in a country where good quality healthcare is costly and mental illness is not readily accepted in society.

I can close my eyes and picture being held up in a queue of traffic and hearing the slightest tap on my window. It's a child, a boy of 7 or 8-years old with his hands moving from his stomach to his mouth, showing his hunger, begging me to do something about it. In my travels, I have come across many street children – and it never stops hurting, it never stops being startling to see a child run after your car shouting 'mama, mama'. I am still a child in many ways, still exploring the world, figuring out my place in it. But to these children, I am a mama with money. I could use my heart and give all that I have to offer, but I choose to use my head to question whose pocket my Shillings end up in. I seek to use my head to find an alternate more innovate way to make a difference in the lives of these children.

Success is as much driven by the heart as the head, and my heart has found its place at the core of life's moments. When you strip away the complexity of the world, all you are left with are moments. And a moment – whether filled with happiness or pain – is the most beautiful gift of all.

January 3, 2012

My new year's resolution

As I grapple this year with setting New Year's resolutions, the crux of confusion lies not in what I want to do, but rather in who I want to be. Perhaps fittingly after living in East Africa for the last year, the antidote to my befuddlement lies hidden amongst the vast plains and treetops of the Masai Mara.

In 2012...

I want **the focus and drive of a cheetah**, as it crouches its way through the high grasses towards a herd of wildebeest. I envy the cheetah's ability to know what it wants and go after it with swiftness, with skill, with determination. When the cheetah sets its target on a prey, there is absolutely nothing that can derail it. Every cell in his body is consumed by the hunt; it is all he sees, it is all he lives for. It is this relentless hunt, this incessant urge to achieve, to be great that I crave with every fibre of my being.

In a world flooded with clutter and noise, it is those who have the ability to listen that hold an ace up their sleeves. I seek **the giraffe's ability to listen**, for though she was not granted with the gift of sound, she was blessed with the incredible ability to perceive. It is through listening that you begin to understand, and understanding is at the core of making a meaningful difference.

Though I envy the ability to listen, I fear leaving this world without making a sound, without leaving a legacy. When I was wrapped in my sleeping bag camping in the Mara, all I could hear in the distance was **the laughing scowls of hyenas. Their voices echo when no one else can be heard** — and in my field of work, this is a skill that is much needed. I seek to be the voice of those who are not given the power to speak, to take a stand when no else does. I strive to leave this Earth having made a sound; to forget about the need to be liked and the need to fit in, to embody **the authenticity of a zebra**, whose stripes are unlike anyone that has existed or will ever exist. To be me.

I strive to exude **the confidence of a lion** as he struts his prowess through the Mara. His presence commands attention, it commands respect simply by being who he is, who he  was born to be. But rather than that confidence be mistaken for ego, I seek **the grace and simplicity of a gazelle**. Though she is small, she emanates beauty and elegance with every step that she takes. She is radiant.

Working in rural Kenyan communities, I have learned that it really does not take much to be happy. Life is not all about Porches and designer suits — it's about a sense of community. I seek **the acceptance of the wildebeest** who migrate from the Serengeti to the Mara every year joining herds of 1.5 million others. Different localities, different families — none of that matters, because at the end of the day, they are all one.

At this particular point in my life, I crave **the freedom of a male impala**, who is accountable to no one but himself and like a leopard, is completely satisfied living a solitary life doing what he pleases, when he pleases it. Eventually, eons and eons down the road, I seek to embody **the maternal instinct of any mother found in the Masai Mara**. Whether it is the elephant who carries her baby for 22 months and feeds for up to two years after birth or the Thomson gazelle who separates from her pack for several years to raise her baby — teaching it how to defend itself, teaching it how to feed — before re-joining the rest of the family. It is this selflessness, this ability to love someone more than life itself that I hope to acquire wholeheartedly.

I wish **to age gracefully like a crocodile** who is one of the longest living creatures in the Mara, enjoying the beauty of life for seventy to a hundred years before becoming one with the Earth again.

The Mara is a fruit salad of emotions. Of focus and drive; of confidence, authenticity, freedom; of listening; of grace and simplicity; of selflessness, acceptance and love. In 2012, I seek to achieve this balance. This is my resolution.

January 18, 2012

From ideas to impact

For the last 6 months, I have spent countless hours looking at social innovations in primary health care settings in Kenya. I have come across leading organizations harnessing the capabilities of entrepreneurs in rural communities. I have read case studies on the next 'big thing' in water purification, alternative energy and agriculture, and listened to hours' worth of Ted Talks on the challenges faced by developing economies.

It is abundantly clear that there is no shortage in this world of brilliant people with brilliant ideas. Innovation and out-of-the-box thinking are common-speak amongst today's generation of go-getters. But what is equally clear is it's not all about the idea. Sure, a fancy new gadget can attract donor funding. Sure, a malnourished child holding a tech-savvy tool makes for a compelling photo on an NGO's promotional material. But the stuff that really matters — the stuff behind the idea — is what defines the success of a project. Most of development work is uncannily unsexy. But that's where you get to roll up your sleeves, throw yourself into the nitty gritty and do some real thinking. And that's where I think the fun really begins.

But for most, the fun begins much earlier, in a well-polished boardroom table with suited colleagues who develop a product based on superficial notions of what a rural community in East Africa needs. An eloquently prepared PowerPoint deck showcases expected yields on a quarterly basis for the next 3 years, and suits adjourn the meeting visualizing this as the turning point for the NGO suffering from donor fatigue or as the gold-standard in corporate social responsibility.

But then the innovation begins its implementation phase and things don't seem to operate according to the colourful line graphs developed in a city thousands of miles away. Supply chains are faulty because of lack of maintenance of the one ambulance operating in the village. Male-dominated households prevent the product from reaching its target of women and children. People place more value on their chickens than a flashy device that holds no promise of putting food on the table or paying for school fees. And that's when you rely on the unsexy stuff. That's when you admit to failure and spend a day in the field with a farmer understanding his major challenges. That's when you shadow a nurse at a village dispensary to observe her overtaxed task-list and obstacles of providing good quality care. It's not just about the idea. It's about the ability to listen to what people really need and understand how that idea fits into their values, their cultures, their lives. It's about having the tact to observe inefficiencies and suggest simple, practical, cost-effective solutions.

And once you begin to understand the gap and potential, that's when you engage with the government to brainstorm how that idea is aligned with their strategic plan to ultimately ensure community ownership and sustainability. All too often, we judge governments in developing countries as corrupt and revert to creating our own parallel structures. Granted, parallel health structures for example, are necessary to prove the efficacy of a new innovation, to take a risk in a generally risk-averse area. But they are only sustainable if at some defined point, they merge into the infrastructure that currently exists. The infrastructure that we as aid organizations should seek to improve, rather than developing new competing structures. And that requires talking. That requires listening. By observing, by conversing, we begin to shift the focus from a 'donor agency - implementing agency' feedback loop to an 'implementing agency – community' feedback loop. A structure that puts the beneficiaries back in the driving seat where they belong.

What I've learned is that even when you have the idea, the one that's going to get you on the cover of Times magazine, the potential for change is limited unless you sit back, shut up, and listen to what communities really need. Sustainable development requires engagement with communities beyond the surface-level, it requires the building of mutually-beneficial relationships and asking critical questions about the underlying system in place. Because at the end of the day, an innovation is just a nicely packaged idea, unless it goes beyond the glamorous surface of cover photos and success stories and tackles the messy, muddled matters at the core of the issue.

January 23, 2012

The only thing worse than the smell of a dead rat is...

...not knowing where it is. I can sadly say this with conviction, for I have been joined by a family of rats over the last week in my Nairobi flat. Big, black, furry rodents with tails that double their size. As I worked at the dining room table, I could see them stirring out of the corner of my eye, scurrying between the stove and refrigerator and back again. They pitter-pattered across the linoleum floor throughout the night and left their waste wheresoever they pleased. A day after they took stock in my flat, the maintenance crew arrived — good intentions in one hand, kryptonite in the other — and strategically placed poison throughout the house. Brilliant idea, ingenious really. Until the rats consumed the poison and died in undisclosed locations around the flat, leaving an increasingly deadly stench. So back again the maintenance crew came, superbly eager and on a mission to solve the mysterious case of the missing rats. They looked left, they looked right. They looked up, they looked down. They moved every kitchen appliance, but the intruders were nowhere to be found. It was a Saturday evening and with reassuring faces, the crew recommended using air freshener to dissipate the smell while we wait for them to return next week during regular working hours. They marched out of the front door leaving us with a floor full of dust from overturned appliances, a swarm of flies and an unbearably wretched stench.

The situation is less than desirable but it certainly sums up my experience with traditional approaches to development. A far reach I know, but please bear with me.

We approach communities in need — sometimes because we are called upon (as we called the maintenance men), sometimes without a request, and arrive on scene with the best of intentions. There is no doubt in our minds that we are going to solve this, we are going to help those who need it, we are going 'to save Africa'. We design and implement an intervention — lay down our own poisons if you will — and pat ourselves on the back for a job well done as we walk confidently away. The problem is every action has a consequence, which brings about a host of new challenges requiring its own set of solutions. Dead rats because of a poison we planted — or in the case of community development, increased gender inequalities because of an irrigation system we installed that favours a traditionally male-dominated sector; or designing a water collection mechanism that no longer requires women to fetch water, thereby devaluing their role in the community without providing an alternative means to be engaged in society. These are by-products of our initial inputs and yet, most times we fail to take accountability for the domino effect of issues and wipe our hands clean of the mess.

Sometimes we go back — like my well-intentioned maintenance crew — to finish what we had a hand in starting. When we go back, the complexity of the problem necessitates turning to new tools, or redefining the uses of the tools we generally use. And when those don't work, or we lack the funds to invest in new resources, we turn our attention to other matters with the promise of coming back. And that's our problem. Too few organizations go back. Instead, we intricately design a report that highlights our successes and justifies our failures and move on to implement the same intervention in another area. Something Einstein would deem as insanity.

This is what has happened to the state of Africa, according to Dambisa Moyo's telling book "Dead Aid". We resolved to help those in need by providing financial assistance to Africa in the 1950s after seeing the success of the approach in re-building a ravaged European economy post-WWII. In the 1970s with soaring prices of oil, we sought to help the poor by lending millions of dollars to the most un-creditworthy countries — and then provided poverty-related aid when these African countries found themselves in greater debt trying to pay back past loans. Aid, deceptively, is not free. The interest payments further pushed Africa into a downward spiral of poverty, which again we sought to fix by lending money to defaulting nations to help them repay what they owed through an IMF initiative called structural adjustment. This served to increase African countries' aid-dependence and throw them into a larger pool of debt. Our initial intervention created a domino effect of problems — and we repeatedly turned to the same approach to fix these problems. We are now in a state of having spent $300 billion of development assistance in Africa over the last 40 years with many poverty indicators remaining stagnant (including life expectancy), and some even worse than when we first arrived — with good intentions of course.

And now that many African countries are suffering from high disease burden, low literacy rates and limited infrastructure, we supply free condoms and bed nets — the band-aid air freshener approach — and promise to come back another time when it is more convenient to our schedules, to our interests. We walk away, leaving behind a mass of problems for an ill-equipped, ill-resourced community to deal with.

To catch the rat, to solve the problems of ultra-poverty, it takes the perfect mix of ingredients and a precise recipe tailored towards the context. I think development has failed because we have failed to achieve that perfect mix. Sometimes we over-emphasize the importance of financial assistance and forget the merit of impact investment. Sometimes we pay more attention to monitoring and evaluation plans rather than spending dedicated time in communities to observe the impact made. What the perfect community development recipe dictates, I alone cannot answer. You cannot answer. Creating a thoughtful, innovative, effective recipe requires an equally important mix of chefs with different expertise; it requires a multi-sectoral approach where the beneficiaries are just as equally seen and heard in the kitchen as the agency providing the money. If we can do this, if brilliant minds from the private, NGO, educational, government sectors can collaborate with communities to develop locally-driven, context-based recipes with defined and measurable outcomes — and have the persistence and creativity to tweak the recipe when things don't work out as planned — then I have hope that sustainable development is possible. Sustainable development is within reach. Sustainable development can happen in our lifetime.

Until then, I seek to develop a locally-driven, context-based recipe with defined and measurable outcomes to rid of my current rat friends. Multi-sectoral and stakeholder input are welcomed and much appreciated.

March 20, 2012

The next generation of social entrepreneurs

On Sunday March 18th, while the rest of the world was in bed recovering from St. Patty's Day partying, 50 students were in a lecture theatre at the University of Waterloo in Ontario, Canada, talking about social development. The Build-a-Change Symposium, an initiative developed by Smart Solutions Inc., challenged students to brainstorm ideas to real-world problems faced in the development sector, and pitch their ideas to a panel of judges. As one of the judges, it was a joy to see passionate youth from different disciplines take the knowledge they have learned in the classroom and apply it towards challenges faced on the ground. In many ways, the symposium was a source of immense hope.

My love affair with the development sector began as a wide-eyed youth who had every intention of wanting to 'save the world'. There were inequities that existed; I was privileged to be born into a life of opportunity; I felt like I needed to do something about. It was as simple as that.

During my first few weeks living and working in Coastal Kenya, I was enamoured by the new cultures, the languages, the freedom to explore, the opportunity to make a difference. I was hopelessly idealistic that if I worked hard enough, that if I spent day and night understanding the problems of Africa, I could find a way to make everything better. I could make all the inequities disappear and transform these communities into places of opportunity for all those living within. But once the honeymoon period passed, the challenges of this transformation became abundantly clear. As a sector, we're constantly challenged by limited resources — funding seems to be dwindling each year, meaning there are fewer dollars available to serve an ever-growing population. The structure of project grants, varying from 3-5 years, compromises the long-term sustainability of an initiative. The involvement of communities throughout the duration of a project cycle — from the needs assessment to implementation to evaluation — is limited. Silo mentalities persist in spite of the clear need for multi-sector input approaches to community development. Collaboration amongst stakeholders in a given area is limited equating to inefficiencies in resources and overburdening existing community structures such as Community Health Workers. Measuring impact in a cost-effective, reliable way seems to be the million dollar question that we have yet to answer.

But in all of these challenges lay glimmers of hope. And my experience at the Build-a-Change Symposium was a major source of hope. To see youth who are passionate about social development, who have a restless desire to make a difference. University students who are less concerned about salaries and benefits, and are instead contemplating careers that have the potential to make a meaningful impact. Tech-savvy youth who understand the role technology can play in facilitating change.

This is the next generation of young social entrepreneurs that are ready to hit the stage. They're innovative, passionate, global-minded and addicted to achievement. If given the opportunity and guidance, there is no telling the impact this generation could have.

Epilogue

After frequent back-and-forth visits from Kenya to Canada, I permanently moved back home in May 2012 to take care of my Mom who was recently diagnosed with two types of blood cancer.

The transition back to North American life has been interesting, and I often feel foreign in my own city. A perplexing thought given that for more than two decades, this was the only life I knew. Now, I find shopping malls overwhelming and question the way we swipe a credit card without a second thought. The luxuries of a cashless society and the constant state of 'want' fascinate me. When I first arrived, I instinctively locked my car doors and held my purse close to my body when walking on the streets — I forgot what it was like to live in a safe place. I am constantly amazed by the high prices of groceries and surprised when I cannot barter down the prices — even in a Kenyan accent that I have apparently begun to adorn. I am saddened by children who have forgotten to learn how to play and who grow up knowing nothing but a life of excess. I find myself walking slower, enjoying the process of getting somewhere rather than simply being in a rush to get there. I unfortunately am late all the time — a bad habit I have picked up in Africa that I plan to change. Eventually. I strive to create the same feeling of an abundance of time that I experienced in Africa. To make my days stretch into an eternity; for here, it almost seems like we have fewer hours in the day.

My experience in East Africa was a starting point of a long career I see for myself in the development sector. There are many more lessons to be learned, novel approaches to be tried and new communities to engage with. There are questions of sustainability and scale that still require answers, and tools of measuring impact that have yet to be developed. As I close this chapter of my life, I look to the future with great excitement, for my journey through international development has only just begun!

About the Author

Sabrina Natasha Premji is a recipient of the International Development Management Fellowship, awarded by the Aga Khan Foundation Canada and Canadian International Development Agency. In 2010, she was placed with the Community Health Department, Aga Khan Health Service, in Mombasa, Kenya. The following year, Sabrina moved to Nairobi, Kenya to work as the Project Manager of an Integrated Primary Health Care Start-Up Project, a collaboration between the Aga Khan University, University of California San Francisco and Ministries of Health (Coast Province, Kenya).

Sabrina holds an Honours Bachelor of Science degree from McMaster University, with a double minor in Psychology and Health Studies. She is currently based in Toronto, Canada.

Continue to follow Sabrina on her travels: www.sabrinapremji.com